FLEA MARKET
STYLE

FLEA MARKET
STYLE

DECORATING
WITH A CREATIVE EDGE

EMELIE TOLLEY
and CHRIS MEAD

Clarkson Potter/Publishers
NEW YORK

ALSO BY EMELIE TOLLEY AND CHRIS MEAD

Herbs: Gardens, Decorations, and Recipes
Cooking with Herbs
Gifts from the Herb Garden
The Herbal Pantry
A Potpourri of Pansies
Gardening with Herbs
Tulips

PUBLISHED BY CLARKSON N. POTTER, INC.,
201 East 50th Street, New York, New York 10022.
Member of the Crown Publishing Group.
Random House, Inc. New York, Toronto, London, Sydney, Auckland
www.randomhouse.com

CLARKSON N. POTTER, POTTER, and colophon are trademarks
of Clarkson N. Potter, Inc.

Printed in China

DESIGN BY JILL ARMUS

Library of Congress Cataloging-in-Publication Data
Tolley, Emelie. Flea market style: decorating with a
creative edge / Emelie Tolley and Chris Mead. Includes index.
1. House furnishings. 2. Interior decoration. 3. Flea markets.
I. Mead, Chris. II. Title.
TX311.T65   1998
645—dc21   97-35937

ISBN 0-517-70167-7

10 9 8 7 6 5 4 3 2 1
First Edition

TO MY MOTHER, Doreen, for her sense
of fun and her positive outlook on life,
and my father, Fred, for his artistic talents.
—C.P.M.

═══════

TO CHRIS, for his unerring eye and his
ability to always look beyond the obvious to
make every book better. —E.T.

ACKNOWLEDGMENTS

═══════

WE ARE GRATEFUL to the many people who have helped us put this book together and especially those who were kind enough to let us photograph their houses and their individual takes on flea market style: Mary Baltz, Bobby Bant, Jeannie Blake, Joan Burstein, Peter Cicero, Rebecca Cole, John Derian, Andrea Dern, Alexander Exarchos, Tom Fallon, Phyllis Lande Fairhurst, Berns Fry, Jill Gill, Tracy Gill and Simeon Lagodich, Sandy and John Horvitz, Wallace Hunting, Alexander Jakowec and Alex Sigmon, Donna Karan, Albert Morris, Ellen O'Neill, Christina Redding, Thomas Rosamilia, Ruby Beets Antiques, Kathy Shorr, Beverly Silver, Hunt Slonem, Rawley Sorman, Diana White. Many also gave us ideas on where to photograph and how to tackle a day at the flea market. So did James Cramer and Dean Johnson, Margaret Walsh, Sharone Einhorn, Mary Emmerling, Kevin Maple, Masako Maruyama, Matthew Mead, Kirk Moore, Eleanor Kennedy, Barbara Remia, Kathleen Scupp, Honey Wolters, and Henro, Sammy's Antiques and C.I.T.E. in New York City. Dealers from Brimfield to the Rose Bowl allowed us to photograph their booths and shared their knowledge of the market with us. And as always, all our friends at Clarkson Potter have worked unstintingly to make this book a reality, especially our ever-patient and attentive editor, Pam Krauss; Margot Schupf, who was always there when needed; Jill Armus, who transformed text and photographs into a handsome book. We thank you.

CONTENTS

INTRODUCTION

LIKE MILLIONS of others, Chris Mead and I often spend our free time browsing through flea markets. Whether a few vendors set up in a field or a sprawling collection of dealers installed on acres of land, these open-air markets provide an irresistible opportunity to search out hidden treasure. Many of us cut our collector's teeth in Europe's enticing old markets: Portobello Road and Bermondsey in London, Porta Por-tunese in Rome, La Rastro in Madrid, and, of course, Le Marché aux Puces in Paris, which is said to have been named for the flea-infested furniture often found there. Recently, however, flea markets, outdoor "antiques" fairs, and even tag sales have proliferated on city streets and coun-try roads. Today most of us need travel no more than a mile or two to join the hunt for an object that beckons to us with its

beauty, whether it's a naive painting or an old balustrade. This urge to acquire is hardly a recent advent. Much like today's collectors, Renaissance shoppers sought out whatever they found beautiful: art, furniture, even architectural remnants. Whether an object was new or old mattered less than that it pleased their eye. Eventually, however, as valuable possessions were passed from one generation to another, collecting antiques became a serious business, especially in America. Up until the end of World War II collectors were those who invested in major antiques: The homes of wealthy Americans were more apt to resemble a museum than a comfortable place to live. It wasn't until war's end that decorating lightened up and collecting as we know it began. Although an antique by definition continued to be an object at least a hundred years old, the term no longer referred only to fine furniture, art, silver, and porcelain. Younger people began buying less serious "antiques." The objects may have been of the required vintage, but instead of coming from rich homes, they reflected the simpler needs of country life. Quilts, painted furniture, folk art, and stoneware all became popular quarry for collectors. Gradually, the line between antique and collectible was blurred and folksy objects from the turn of the century were added to the mix. As the years went by, interest in Victoriana grew, and from there it was only a small step to Art Deco and beyond. Now most but certainly not all of the collectibles that show up at flea markets were produced after 1920, allowing us to indulge in nostalgia—and often good design—at reasonable prices. Lower prices prevail for some older pieces, too, because dealers have less overhead at flea markets and auctions than they would at an upscale store—in fact, you may well find yourself in competition with a shop owner for a piece intended for resale at a hefty mark-up. ◆ Fortunately for the collector, there are thousands of recognized markets across the country in addition to small local affairs. Some major markets, such as Brimfield in Massachusetts, have shows just three times a year, but they are weeklong blockbusters with thousands of dealers displaying an amazing array of merchandise. Others take place once a month, biweekly, or every weekend. These established shows are augmented by thousands of yard and estate sales that are a terrific introduction to collecting because things are generally affordable. Their reasonable prices can allow you to start a collection and build up confidence before you progress to the flea market and dealers. ◆ People everywhere have taken to flea market shopping with zeal, giving rise to a subculture of avid collectors who have

In Chris's apartment a beautifully detailed, appealingly aged architectural remnant that once adorned a gracious building doubles as a piece of sculpture.

Chris provided daylight for a windowless bathroom by installing an interior window that can be covered with a pair of French shutters for privacy. A hundred-year-old pine door was turned into a space-saving pocket door.

turned "going to the flea" into a national pastime. New devotees are discovering the exhilaration, sociability, and pleasure of the chase each week. Since entrance fees are modest or nonexistent and the markets are generally in the open air, they offer an inexpensive way to spend the day outdoors. And, more than likely, you'll have the added diversion of chatting with friends and favorite dealers. But above all, there is the lure of the hunt, the possibility that right up until the very last minute you might uncover that special treasure. ◆ There are other compelling reasons to get caught up in flea market mania. With shoppers in every category looking for bargains, flea markets offer unbeatable prices even in these days of discount shopping. Old sofas and chairs, for example, will probably be better made than pricier new models from a department store and can be re-covered to suit your decor. The perfect fabric for the job might show up among another dealer's wares. Even the most expensive flea market pieces generally cost less than a comparable new piece bought at retail—and the hunt is much more fun. Consider, too, your contribution to the environment. When older goods are recycled, fewer trees are cut down for furniture, fewer chemicals are used to make fabrics, and less energy is used in manufacturing kitchenware. ◆ Another advantage of flea market shopping over department store decorating is an undeniably personal result. A slight imperfection in a piece adds a sense of history that is invariably more interesting than the bland uniformity of newly manufactured pieces; a quirky mirror or chair can give a room distinction that just can't be found at retail. Adding just a single piece of furniture with a worn finish to a more traditional room enlivens the entire scheme. Rely on your eye to help you gather an eclectic mix of objects; then rethink how to use them. A beautiful door could just as easily be used as a headboard; a splendid gate makes a sculptural wall decoration. Let the texture of flaking paint or unfinished wood, the sheen of china, the depth of woven surfaces, the patina of metals work together to produce an environment that is uniquely yours. ◆ We decided to write this book to show you how other collectors are using their finds, hoping to inspire you to shop with a keener eye, more imagination, and greater pleasure. Whether you collect postcards or picture frames, Depression glass or vintage clothes, buy architectural remnants to decorate your garden or a '40s tablecloth to use as a bedcover or curtains, are a seasoned marketgoer or an enthusiastic novice, this book will help you derive more pleasure from the hunt and live more creatively with your finds.

Found in many shapes and sizes,

old windows are easily converted to mirrors. Chris uses an oval one next to the front door of his apartment.

Chris has recycled architectural

remnants to provide a dramatic setting for the bed. Two old columns lean against the wall while mirror-filled windows define the space and serve as a headboard.

the
CHASE

ONCE YOU CATCH the flea market bug, there's never an excuse for being bored—at least on weekends. Most Saturdays and Sundays you will find a flea market or an outdoors "antiques" fair in full swing somewhere close by, and there are always yard sales and estate sales to scour as well. Even on vacation or a business trip, chances are you'll discover some sort of flea market or antique show that's worth a visit. Check the local papers for details, or check one of the flea market directories and see page 206 before you leave home. ◆ Pickings vary from market to market. Basic flea markets may offer new merchandise like jeans and

Vintage textiles

and other treasures

entice shoppers on a sunny

day in a Long Island field.

It helps to be
strong when

you buy a piece like this

painted chest.

Old signs of

every sort are highly

collectible.

T-shirts and pots and pans along with a variety of collectibles, secondhand furniture, and the occasional antique tossed casually into the mix; outdoor antique fairs generally have a better grade of merchandise, although not every item is likely to meet the accepted definition of an antique, an object that is more than 100 years old. When a flea market or show moves indoors, the quality (as well as the prices) of the offerings usually goes up. Such events are more costly for the dealers, who may be charged substantial booth fees, as well as for shoppers. In England, an event known as a "boot sale," a gathering of cars in a field with wares displayed in the trunk, inspired by the American forerunner of today's flea markets, is the current rage. This kind of spontaneous event may well regain its popularity on this side of the Atlantic as prices at more established markets rise to reflect vendors' higher costs.

◆ For the truly bargain-conscious and dedicated shopper, yard sales can provide the best opportunities to uncover an overlooked treasure. Although you may have to pick through more junk than at a flea market, prices will surely be lower since there is no middleman involved in the transaction. Frequently owners aren't aware of market values and don't realize the old vase Aunt Agatha gave them is a very collectible piece of American pottery. And yard sales are definitely the best place to find simple utilitarian items. ◆

Estate sales are a good source for larger pieces, especially furniture. They often have a higher grade of merchandise as well as higher prices. Because they are run by people who specialize in the business it's unlikely that a real steal will surface, but you'll still get good value. No inveterate collector ever passes thrift and consignment shops by, since people who haven't the time or inclination to run a yard sale send their clutter to these outlets where they are often sold at rock bottom prices. To outwit the dealers who visit them on a regular basis, find out which day new merchandise is put out on the floor. And don't forget to check the dump if there is one in your community. In this age of recycling, most have a special section for major castoffs where you might find anything from a garden chair to a wonderful old terra-cotta pot. The adage "one man's trash is another man's treasure" is never more apt than when applied to collectors.

Weary from a morning of

shopping, flea marketers

rest and refuel around picnic

tables at Brimfield.

FLEA MARKET buffs can generally be separated into two groups: collectors obsessed with finding new additions to their ever-expanding personal collections and those who simply enjoy the chase and consider any find a wonderful bonus. Whichever group you fall into, approach your outing with a spirit of fun and adventure, and always keep your eyes—and mind—open for unexpected discoveries. Here are a few tricks of the trade to make your sortie more pleasurable and rewarding.

WORKING A FLEA

Getting Ready Dress for comfort. This is especially important at a big market where you'll be in the field all day. Wear layers so that if the temperature changes as the day goes on, you can add or subtract sweaters and shirts. If there is any possibility of rain, take a lightweight waterproof poncho, too. Since the fields may be muddy or dusty, wear sturdy, well-fitting shoes that are impervious to either condition. Even at small local fleas where an hour or two is all you need to scout the merchandise, you'll appreciate comfortable shoes. Also dress for visibility. Wearing a brightly colored shirt or hat makes it easier for friends to spot you. ◆ Carry a big bag or a backpack. Since flea market dealers seldom have shopping bags, bringing a satchel of your own and even a few plastic shopping bags makes it easier to carry small purchases with you. Unless you are going to wear a separate waist pouch, make sure the bag has a well-concealed zippered pocket for your money, checkbook, and credit cards. You don't want the day ruined by a pickpocket. ◆ Be prepared to pay in cash (preferably in small denominations). Cash is the preferred medium of exchange, but most dealers will accept checks with proper ID. Credit cards can sometimes be used at the larger, more upscale markets. ◆ Before you leave home make a list of your "wants," and if you're looking for any major pieces of furniture, mirrors, or other large pieces, jot down the necessary measurements. It's extremely frustrating to pass up a painted cupboard just like the one you've been searching for because you don't know if it will fit in the space between the windows or clear the ceiling. ◆ If you are working the market with a friend, always agree on a time and place to meet in case you get separated. A pair of walkie-talkies allows serious shoppers to keep in touch and compare

An entrepreneurial home owner

takes advantage of the

Brimfield crowds by staging

her own yard sale along

the roadside.

prices. ◆ Bring the biggest car you can as well as some boxes, bubble wrap, and/or newspaper. A moving blanket is inexpensive and useful for big pieces. And if you are on a mission to furnish an entire room or house, renting a van or truck may be a smart investment. ◆ You can tuck a picnic lunch and something to drink into your bag, but it's just one more thing to carry. Even the smallest shows generally offer coffee, cold drinks, and muffins or a hot dog. At the bigger shows there is greater variety, but the trick is to eat early or late when crowds are at a minimum to save valuable shopping time.

Plan of Attack
Veteran flea market shoppers develop different strategies, but all agree that to get the most out of a show, it's wise to have a plan. ◆ If you are looking for a particular item or are a serious collector, attend preshow "early bird" openings. The higher admission prices are a worthwhile expenditure for first crack at the merchandise.

WHAT TO BRING WITH YOU

A tape measure and small notebook and pen for recording your wish list and furniture dimensions.

A flashlight for early-morning shows. It's not always easy to see markings or the condition of a piece in the dim morning light.

A magnifying glass, especially if you're buying pottery and silver. It makes checking marks much easier.

A receipt book. Many dealers don't have them and if you make a big purchase, you'll want a written receipt.

Sunglasses, sunscreen, and a hat. The sun gets brutally hot in the middle of an open field.

A reliable price guide. It can help you make buying decisions if you are uncertain about what market values are.

Gently used toys, kitchenware, and glass and china are among the offerings at Ranconcas Woods on a fall Sunday.

A charming vignette catches the eye of flea market buffs.

At an outdoor show in the Netherlands, architectural remnants sit side by side with an old window.

This Brimfield dealer offers an eclectic mix. The toy car will probably be snapped up and then refurbished by a collector.

◆ If getting the best prices is paramount, attend the last few hours of the show. Given the vagaries of fashion and individual taste, it's entirely possible that the item of your dreams could still be waiting for a buyer and the dealer may be willing to take less to avoid packing it up for the trip home. ◆ Work the show in an organized way so you don't miss any dealers. Go around the edges, then up and down the center aisles—or start at one end and go up and down the aisles. The exception: If you are looking for a particular item and know certain dealers are most likely to have it, head for them first, then go back and work the rest of the show. ◆ Some collectors prefer to do a quick walk-through of the entire show before buying; others buy as they go. If you are looking for a special item, the quick walk-through has an obvious advantage: It prevents the unwelcome surprise of finding an item similar to one you've bought for less or spending all your money before coming upon the one thing you must have. However, there's no guaranteeing items will be there when you return. ◆ If you buy as you go, pay for your treasure and ask the dealer to hold it. Most are happy to do this: Just be sure to get a receipt and make a note of the booth number or location so you can find it again. Keep a list of what you bought so you don't forget to collect anything. At the end of the day, you can often drive the car onto the field to pick up big purchases. ◆ Take time to look at each booth carefully. Sometimes a treasure is tucked behind another object or under a table. And casually check what other people are holding; they are likely to put it down without buying. By the same token, keep items you plan on buying in your hand or risk losing them to another buyer. ◆ Even if you are collecting something very specific, look at booths that offer a potpourri of merchandise. You'll often find the best prices there because the dealers don't know what they have. New dealers also often ask lower prices. Unless you're an expert, don't approach collecting as an investment. Predicting the collectibles is just as tricky as playing the stock market. ◆ Look at everything creatively. Although most items have an obvious use, remember that old shutters can be fashioned into a decorative screen, an old silver belt buckle could become a beautiful pin, and an old eggbeater might stand in for a piece of kitchen sculpture.

TO BECOME A PRO

T HE PROPER EQUIPMENT and a good strategy alone won't ensure a successful day at the flea market: You must go home with a treasure. If you are a novice, look for affordable objects that speak to you in a particular way and could be the start of a collection. Before you spend lots of money on a flea market purchase, however, become an educated buyer by developing an eye for good design, a sense of quality, some general knowledge of prices, and a bit of expertise in the area of your choice. It's easier than you think. ◆ Visit museums, fine antiques stores, and auction houses. This exposure to finer examples of furniture and decorative objects will teach your eye to distinguish good lines and proportions, superior workmanship, and quality materials. ◆ Study prices at shows, in shops, in auction catalogs, and in newspapers published for the antiques trade to get a sense of what prices you may encounter and help you spot a bargain. ◆ Read home magazines to learn about new trends and imaginative uses of objects in decorating and books on design to learn about traditional furnishings and decorative objects. ◆ Old magazines from the '50s and '60s may offer an idea of what the next trend might be. ◆ Talk to dealers. If they're not busy, most are delighted to share their knowledge, as are other collectors. They can tell you what's hot, what to look for, how to spot fakes. ◆ Keep in mind that items that reflect a historical event or a particular culture or aesthetic are generally more desirable. So is well-designed handwork of any kind, an example of a breakthrough in technology, or a signed piece. ◆ Each item has its own subjective worth if you're buying for pleasure and not investment purposes. If you love something and it fits into your lifestyle, buy it, collect it, enjoy it. ◆ Once you decide what you are going to collect, buy a book devoted to the subject. Only specialized books have enough space to give all the background information you need. ◆ Keep an eye on the book market and the news. Once a book appears on any subject, it immediately becomes more collectible. The publicity surrounding the anniversary of a major event has the same effect.

One Sunday every month crowds

pour into the famed Rose Bowl flea market in Pasadena, where vintage pieces from the '40s and '50s are plentiful.

Thanks to a missing seat,

this shopper is able to sling his rocking chair over his shoulders.

Trash or treasure?

Sometimes it takes a sharp eye to uncover a find.

ONCE YOU DECIDE TO BUY

◆ Don't hesitate. Buy anything you can't live without on the spot; you may not get another chance.

◆ Don't head right for the item you covet. Ask about several before negotiating for the one you really want.

◆ Ask questions and look the piece over carefully for repairs and signs of wear. Remember that there are many reproductions out there.

◆ Bargain, but do it nicely. No dealer will object to your asking "Is this your best price?" or "Can you do better on this?" but don't make an insultingly low offer or tell him your opinion of what it's worth or how you've seen a similar item for less elsewhere. When you buy several pieces from the same dealer, he will be more inclined to give a discount. Big pieces that are more trouble to pack up may also be more negotiable.

◆ Paying cash for an expensive piece may also lead to a discount. Rain, unbearable heat, or a slow show can all favorably affect prices.

◆ Remember, flea market purchases can go into the thousands of dollars and still be a bargain com-pared to the same item bought in a retail store. In the end, buying objects of superior quality, even if they're expensive, will be a good investment. Always get full written documentation of age and provenance on a receipt for expensive items. If a dealer refuses to put the information in writing, you can be sure it isn't true.

◆ Don't buy something just to have a souvenir or because you lost something you really wanted to another shopper. You will invariably be unhappy with these purchases once you get them home.

PURELY DECORATIVE

Using an object in an unpredictable way always makes it more interesting. Ellen O'Neill admired this old sink's handsome lines and envisioned it as a decorative piece of "sculpture" for the entryway of her country house.

THERE IS A TROVE of decorative treasures waiting to be discovered at flea markets if you approach the hunt with imagination and an open mind. The potential of a glittering chandelier or a shell-encrusted mirror is obvious, but a creative flea market buff looks far beyond the obvious and, seeing a piece of architectural woodwork or a porcelain sink, spots decorative possibilities in the item that bear no relationship to its original purpose. Other flea marketers prize the items that dealers refer to as "smalls" on their own merits, amassing collections of such seemingly mundane items as license plates, toy horses, razors, and marbles. Where smalls are

concerned every true flea market shopper knows "more is better"; while one or two of these items might seem ordinary or even uninteresting, grouped in multiples and handsomely displayed they make a major decorative statement. ◆ This chapter highlights some typical decorative collectibles that are still readily available, generally at prices that range from reasonable to downright cheap.

Barbershop Memorabilia

In the past few years, collectors have begun searching out old razors with handles made of exotic materials such as bone, buffalo horn, mother-of-pearl, sterling silver, or ivory. Even plain celluloid handles are of interest when decorated with an image. ◆ Neck brushes and decorative bottles, in which barbers kept lotions, hair tonics, and colognes, and personalized shaving mugs maintained by barbers for their customers are also good finds.

Cameras
Early cameras were often complicated mechanisms used primarily by professionals, but with the advent of

Shaving brushes

with handles of Bakelite or wood are very collectible, especially when made from badger hair.

Old cameras in all their shapes

and sizes make handsome and interesting displays. Condition is a key factor in value, even with less-expensive models, the exception being unusual or obscure models or those with historic significance.

Demand for
Bakelite jewelry,

especially Art Deco pieces,

has spawned hard-to-detect

reproductions, so buy from

a reputable dealer.

Inexpensive bits
and pieces

can be used to decorate

frames and other objects; a

single earring becomes a tac

pin with the proper findings;

a long string of beads,

a belt or hatband.

Eastman's inexpensive Brownie camera, photography came to the masses. Since then, models have been introduced one after the other, creating a wealth of affordable collectibles. ◆ Camera collecting began in earnest in the United States around 1970, when the first books on the subject appeared. Until then, the original manufacturers' catalogs and advertisements were the only sources of information on old cameras.

Jewelry
Jewelry, ranging from fine old antique pieces to odds and ends of costume jewelry, is abundant at all flea markets. Among the most popular are those of Bakelite and other colored plastics that were molded, carved, and polished to make bangles, pins, necklaces, and earrings. ◆ Costume jewelry from the '30s through the '70s is also in demand, particularly signed pieces by such manufacturers as Richelieu, Trifari, Napier, Eisenberg, Kenneth Jay Lane (KJL), Miriam Haskell, Weiss, as well as any French couturiers.

Surprisingly, a
plastic radio in
working order is not necessarily
of greater value; collectors
rarely play their radios for fear
the heat will crack the material.
The most decorative of these
earlier radios and most appealing to collectors are the colorful
Catalin plastic models from the
'30s and '40s, which could take
any color and be molded into
any shape without burning.

Vintage Radios Most large flea markets boast a vast
array of radios. Those from the 1920s to the '50s are the
most sought after and the most decorative, especially modern Art Deco styles and novelty designs in a range of colored
plastic. Other categories include cathedral radios (vertical
wooden cabinets with a rounded or peaked top reminiscent
of a cathedral window), large floor models known as con-
soles, smaller models for a tabletop, portables designed to be
carried from place to place, and novelty radios shaped like
footballs, cars, or other popular icons. ◆ As these older
radios become increasingly scarce, transistor radios from the
'50s and '60s are becoming collectible. They are particularly
appealing because of their flashy, colorful styling. Color
affects price, and marbleized versions are rarest. The year
1957 brought the first imported transistor, Japan's Sony TR-
63, unleashing a flood of inexpensive models. Look for those
made before 1963 in good condition and with Civil Defense
on the dial at 640 or 1240.

In 1952 Breyer introduced a line of toy horses that have now become collectibles. For people who prefer dogs to horses, they also made small domestic animals. In either case, condition and rarity are important in setting the price.

If toys are in good condition, have an original label, or are in their original box, their value increases markedly.

Marble collectors look for both vintage and Modern Art glass marbles. Along with the marbles themselves, some collectors also look for bags, board games, artwork with children playing marbles, and sets in boxes.

TOYS APPEAL TO the child in all of us. Their age can often be determined by the materials used. Painted tin toys were popular from 1840 to 1900, lithographed tin from 1940 to 1960. Cast-iron toys were made from 1870 to 1930, celluloid toys from 1905 to 1930. ◆ Model trains and cars are some of the most collectible. Train buffs concentrate on cars made between 1870 and 1940, and the bigger the cars, the better. With toy cars, on the other hand, size is of no importance. Any pre-1930 toy car is valuable, as are Matchbox cars, made from the '40s through the '60s when they were packaged in tiny boxes. Although there were never more than seventy-five models on sale at any one time, they were constantly updated, resulting in more than ten thousand models, plus those from specialty lines. Production variations in paint color and decals add to the choice. Limited editions are more valuable, of course. ◆ When buying toys as an investment, make sure all the moving parts work, no pieces are missing, and the paint is original.

TOYS

OLLECTIBLE DOLLS come in many guises, from early 1900s bisque dolls to Shirley Temple and the phenomenal Barbie. Antique dolls are those more than seventy-five years old; modern dolls are from twenty-five to seventy-five years old; all others are considered contemporary. Any doll is more valuable if still in its original box and near mint condition. Good hair, original clothes, and accessories add value. An alert flea market shopper might even stumble upon an elaborately dressed old doll that doubled as a fashion display for traveling clothes salesmen. ◆ Manufacturers also made some black dolls, which are especially collectible.

DOLLS

Teddy Bears

Popular lore says the first teddy bear, made in Brooklyn in 1902, was inspired by a political cartoon of Teddy Roosevelt. The following year, Steiff began manufacturing bears in Germany that captivated an American buyer. Four years later they had produced nearly a million bears and, as other German manufacturers followed suit, that country became the center of teddy bear manufacturing. Although there are still vintage teddy bears about, they are expensive and reproductions abound. Older bears can be distinguished by natural wear, a woven thread nose, and tiny glass shoe button eyes. Later, regular glass eyes were used, and in the '50s and '60s plastic eyes and rubber or plastic noses became the norm. Even more telltale is the look of the bear itself. If you find a bear with a humpback, long arms, and a long muzzle, it probably dates from before 1945. Miniature bears are also collectible and far less expensive.

Materials are the best earmarks of a bear's age: The earliest bears were covered with wool mohair, which gave way to artificial silk plush around 1930. Cotton plush was used after World War II, and from the '50s on, synthetic plush took over.

Although old dolls in good condition are expensive, dolls with missing parts, or the parts themselves, can often be found at low prices and reassembled.

HOW TO CARE FOR DOLLS

TREAT CHINA and bisque dolls gently. Use a soft child's toothbrush and a 50/50 solution of detergent and water to gently scrub away the grime; the paint is fired on, so it is permanent. Rinse off all the detergent with clean water. For day-to-day care, dust carefully.

Keep composition dolls out of direct sunlight and away from heating vents.

Ignore fine crazing, hairline cracks, and minor defects, but be sure to go to a professional to have the paint touched up or major cleaning and repairs done on any doll.

DOLL TOPIARY

With a little creativity, it is easy to make

charming "topiaries" like those created by Alex Sigmon. An extra head could be fashioned into an appealing hat stand by attaching it to a dowel set on a simple wooden base.

MOVING TO NEW YORK from Key West left Alex Sigmon with a yearning for growing things, a yen he partially satisfied by making faux topiaries with dried flowers. "Then I felt I wanted to use more than flowers," he says. "I love dolls and doll parts and I'd found lots of them at yard sales, so I decided to incorporate them into 'topiaries.'" The first was made from half of a German doll. "She had a moss skirt, which was simply a Styrofoam ball covered in moss," he says. "I set it in an old tin, which also came from the flea market." The result was a charming decoration that was more artwork than topiary. ◆ To create your own doll topiary like the ones here, follow the simple instructions below. The dimensions and amounts of materials will depend on the container and doll part you use. Select an old container that is in nice proportion to the doll pieces. There should be enough room around the piece for moss. Alex frequently adds a bit of decoration to the doll's head or to the moss surrounding it, as in the examples in the photographs.

1. Put a layer of sand or stones in the bottom of the container to make it more stable.

2. Join pieces of Styrofoam together with floral picks to create a structure that will fit snugly into the container and protrude above it to the desired height. You will have to cut the Styrofoam and may have to trim the picks as well. For greatest stability, wire the pieces together once the structure is the correct size.

3. Place the Styrofoam in the container. Affix the doll part with a generous amount of hot glue. If the part is particularly heavy, you may want to wire it on as well. Add any other deco-

rations to the doll or to the base with glue, wire, or raffia.

4. Soak enough moss to cover the base around the doll in some plain water. (If you want to green the moss up and make sure it stays green, add a few drops of green food coloring to the water.) Squeeze any excess water from the moss and care- fully arrange it around the doll part so that all the Styrofoam is covered. Attach the moss to the Styrofoam with florist's pins. Allow the moss to dry, then use a glue gun to tack down any stray pieces around the edge if necessary.

ARCHITECTURAL SALVAGE

WHILE ENLIGHTENED communities have begun saving the best of their historic buildings, there are still many less important structures falling prey to the wrecker's ball. But before the real wrecking gets underway, architectural details are often removed to turn up as sculpture, garden decorations, or to be reincorporated into modern interiors. There are dealers for these artifacts in every big city, but columns, tin roof ornaments, old windows and doors, and porch railings also turn up at flea markets. Adding an old door to an all-white interior, installing a mirror in a window frame, or setting a glass tabletop on a handsome capital are a few ways of recycling these pieces. Shutters become room dividers, heavy balustrades reappear as table legs or lamp bases, gargoyles make interesting sculptures, and free-standing columns add drama, define space, and can even substitute as posters for a bed. No matter how you use them, these pieces add character to your rooms.

In this Long Island house, an old iron gate like those displayed above has been salvaged, lined with wire mesh, and reborn as a handsome fireplace screen.

Jill Gill collects bits of old New York buildings because they remind her of her paintings of the city's streets. The glazed fragments are from the old Hotel McAlpin Grill.

Peter Cicero
displays a

handsome carved lintel
from southeast Asia over his
kitchen cabinets. Although
the piece is out of character
with the modern cabinets,
it adds warmth and interest
while the stark white
background focuses
attention on the design.

Dealers offer
a selection of

salvaged cornices that
creative shoppers might use
as shelves or mantels.

OR CENTURIES MAN HAS found the pearly surfaces and intriguing shapes of shells irresistible. They've been admired as an example of nature's extraordinary handiwork; used decoratively to enhance everything from frames to walls; and even been fashioned into folk art figures. As early as the 1500s, collectors sought choice specimens from all parts of the world. Later, still-life painters glorified the best on canvas, and by the 17th century the craze for shells took on manic proportions. While choice specimens were saved for display, more common shells inspired decorative fantasies that ranged from mirrors to entire walls ornamented with intricate patterns in grottoes as well as grand houses. ◆ By the mid 19th century, the Victorian urge to collect and their interest in handwork merged in

SHELL ART

shellwork. Ornamenting boxes, frames, and vases with shells became a favorite ladies' pastime and tourists were entranced with "sailor's valentines," geometric arrangements of tropical shells in shallow wooden octagonal cases. Arranged in sections divided by thin cardboard, the shells in the center section were frequently worked into a customized message. ◆ Shell art of any kind is more desirable if there are no broken or missing shells; an especially good design also adds to the value. If you are buying an expensive piece, have an expert check for replaced shells, and remember that these ornamental shell fantasies are still being made today.

A proprietor of Ruby Beets

Antiques' 1875 Victorian mirror combines natural shells with an ornate form. Overleaf: On a shelf, a series of natural objects shares space with pieces of architectural wood and three striking panels from an Italian orphanage done in the style of Della Robbia's bambini. The shell vase is an example of handicrafts from the '20s or '30s, when pique assiette was popular. More shells decorate the ball atop a balustrade "pedestal" and fill the basket of the '50s chandelier. A portrait of children at the shore doubles here as a colorful way to camouflage a radiator in the summer.

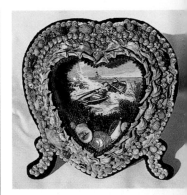

A heart-shaped shell frame is
a good example of this delicate craft.

John Derian's dresser serves as
a showcase for small treasures he has gathered over the years. The shell-covered box and pincushion probably date from the late 19th century.

AN EYE FOR COLOR

ALEX EXARCHOS is a freelance clothing designer whose eye for color and good line is just as evident in the way he decorates his apartment. A perpetual flea market goer, Alex admits he's addicted to objects, but says he is careful to keep his collections in check. "The hardest thing is to edit, to keep to the minimalist faith," he admits. Currently he is searching the markets for colored glass. His interest might be piqued by a piece of Peking glass made in China in the '40s, cased glass made by applying a layer of colored glass to a clear or opalescent base, or an interesting piece of inexpensive glass from the '50s in a shape and color that appeals to his eye. Whatever he buys, he chooses only those pieces in perfect condition, not only to please his own aesthetic but because they are better investments.

While most of his finds come from New York City flea markets, whenever Alex travels on business he tries to shop at the local flea market. A believer in shopping with a mission, he says, "It's easier to look for one thing.

That way you don't spend hours. I go to the market now specifically to look for colored glass, but if something else catches my eye, I stop." Over time, Alex has zeroed in on special dealers that he likes, but always takes time to look through the booths of those who are selling odds and ends. "Even if it's just junk, you can often pick up a good find," he notes. "Sometimes you're more successful when the dealer doesn't specialize in one category." Presently, industrial pieces and office furniture from the early part of the century might cause him to tarry.

Alex Exarchos concentrates on geometric shapes in pure colors—mostly yellows and oranges, although occasionally another color creeps in.

Some of Alex's best pieces, including a big yellow vase and yellow Czechoslovakian bowl, came from Arkansas.

In artist Hunt Slonem's light-filled studio, a collection of birdcages is home to an array of brightly feathered birds that are frequently the subject of his paintings. The ceiling is covered with another collection: old crystal chandeliers from the '40s and '50s that sparkle brightly in the sunlight, out of character but strangely at home in the unadorned work space.

Old glass shades, plentiful and affordable, double as handsome hurricane shades when set on glass plates.

Beverly Silver buys glass candlesticks whenever she sees one she likes. Set on an old piece of lace draped over the living room coffee table, they add flattering light and a romantic note to parties.

F OR YEARS CANDLES were the main source of light, and so candlesticks, especially those from the 19th century, frequently turn up at flea markets in a variety of shapes and materials, including wood, pottery, iron, tin, pewter, brass, and glass. The latter are especially decorative when adorned with crystals, a variation known as a lustre. ◆ Open dishes containing oil and a wick were another early and ineffective form of lighting, but the invention in 1787 of the closed whale-oil lamp resulted in clean, efficient lighting. As whale oil became scarcer, the kerosene lamp took over, and these lamps are now a favorite of collectors; pressed glass examples are still plentiful. Others have hand-painted, ball-shaped shades, but their popularity has encouraged reproductions. ◆ Chandeliers are also found in great variety. Introduced in the mid-17th century, primarily for public spaces like churches and taverns, these unadorned iron or wood models are rare and expensive, but elaborate models of more recent vintage can often be picked up for a surprisingly low price.

LIGHTING

TWIG CHANDELIER

An assortment of old

crystals glitter seductively on a dealer's table, waiting to be used as a replacement on an elaborate chandelier or on a lustre. A more imaginative shopper might buy the inexpensive odd crystals to glitter brightly on a fanciful twig chandelier.

TO ADD SPARKLE to a special evening, find an interesting branch sturdy enough to support several votives and crystals and make a version of this twig chandelier. While you might not want to have this whimsical fixture installed permanently, once you have made it, it's an easy matter to store it away in readiness for another occasion.

1. Prune the branch if necessary to improve the shape. Paint a 2-inch collar of white glue around the large end of the branch, then wrap it with the twine, leaving a long enough tail to tie the branch to a ceiling hook.

2. Wrap wire around the top of each votive, leaving 3 to 4 inches to secure it to the branch. Remove the votives from the wire holders and attach the wires to the branch in a pleasing arrangement.

3. Wire the crystals onto the branch in a random pattern near the votives so they'll reflect the light. Replace the votives, place a tea light in each, and light.

A WELL EDITED ROOM

DONNA KARAN discovered flea markets in the early '60s, when on a trip to London she visited the famous Portobello Road market. An excursion to the famed Marché aux Puces in Paris was next, and now almost any weekend finds her scouting flea markets and her favorite antiques stores in the Hamptons looking for pieces that appeal to her aesthetic sense—regardless of their provenance or original use. Some are destined for her house; others spark ideas for the successful fashion empire she runs with her husband, Stephen Weiss, which has recently expanded to include home furnishings.

A frequent traveler, Donna may be inspired by the subtly colored stones of Florence or the sensuous lines of an African bench, and finds that flea market items often evoke her visual memories in a more tactile way. "For someone who is constantly feeding off visual resources, shopping at the flea market is more stimulating than going to a store—and it's easier to see things that speak to me," she

notes. "Looking at an old dress, for example, is better than doing research at the library: you can pick it up and actually see how it was made."

Disciplined by her work as a fashion designer, Donna used the same careful editing to decorate her country house on Long Island's East End. The result is an intriguing collection of pieces reflecting her interest in texture and patina. "Something old has the comfort of an old friend," she says. "New things never have that." Her eclectic eye is as apt to fasten on humble

In one corner of Donna Karan's living room, a panel of mirrors and painted boiserie reflects a collection of weathered sculptures. One of her collection of white-on-white embroidered shawls is draped over the end of a daybed.

Architectural elements

are recycled into bases for a lamp and nearby coffee table.

OVERLEAF:

Throughout the house, windowed

doors help create more intimate spaces in the open plan. A variety of white fabrics, both old and new, provide visual interest while imparting a sense of tranquillity. Antique table linens add a touch of elegance.

objects as on an extraordinary piece. "I like different textures and the contradiction of prices—an object that costs thousands mixed with one that costs $49," she observes.

Gold frames and chairs are tolerated only when they've aged to a warm patina. Celadon, which appeals because "it has an Asian kind of feeling," is the only other touch of color in the otherwise white environment. "I live in white," says Karan, "because to me color is involved with seasons in fashion. In the house I like my color in flowers and people. Anne Klein once gave me some great advice: 'When in doubt, start with a white shell. It's like a blank canvas.'

"The house is really a small space," she says, "but I wanted to live in an outdoor/indoor environment. That's why I've decorated the outside like a living room, and the living room is like outside with lots of windows, glass, and mirrors. The mirrors aren't about vanity but about seeing more. I wanted to eliminate boundaries. Even the doors leaning against the dead wall at the end of the room suggest other entry spaces."

Her husband, a sculptor, was responsible for the modern architecture of the house, while Donna worked on the elegant but welcoming interior. Comfort was her foremost concern. "That's why I like sleigh beds, daybeds, anything reclining," she notes.

An old pair of French doors defines the separation between the living areas without interrupting the flow of space. In the background, another set of doors, their paint appealingly aged, provides a backdrop to a display case filled with treasures from nature.

A birdbath filled with ivy and a collection of straw hats displayed on a Victorian hall rack help bring the outdoors in.

Bathrooms throughout the house have a Mediterranean feeling and have been designed to look old. In one, an antique washstand and bowl have been fashioned into a handsome sink. A handsome example from her collection of mirrors hangs over it. Another hangs unexpectedly behind the tub's curtain, extending the room's boundaries.

SPORTSMEN

EVEN THE MOST confirmed couch potato can look like a true athlete with a little judicious shopping at the flea market: snowshoes, decoys, saddles, crewing oars, and other sporting paraphernalia make handsome decorative accents or create an entire "theme" room to evoke a rugged, active lifestyle. ◆ True sports aficionados collect, too, extending the field to more mundane items like baseball cards and pennants. They even look for scorecards, sports-oriented metal or plastic premium rings, box tops and wrappers, old comic books, sporty labels from foods and tobacco, menus or matches from restaurants owned by sports figures, and novelty radios with a sporting bent. ◆ No matter what team sport interests you—hockey, football, soccer, basketball, or baseball—the collectibles are pretty much the same: balls, jerseys, equipment, programs, ticket stubs, posters, pictures of teams and individual players, cards, and advertising memorabilia, especially when autographed. Remember

Restoring an old bike is relatively easy, and the prestige of owning and peddling a classic is a bit like driving a vintage Rolls. A great many are still out there ready for many more serviceable years.

Among the most exotic collectibles is a vintage stadium seat, but most collectors settle for something smaller, like the baseball gloves and bats that show up at flea markets.

Bobby Bant bought the first of her collection of trophies and loving cups at a yard sale; finding more became an obsession. The cups needn't be perfect. "It's just a look," she says. "Sometimes I polish them; then I let them tarnish again." The various styles and sizes make her display visually interesting; the engraved inscriptions and dates add a sense of history.

Bears that once prowled the woods now stand guard at Brimfield.

that items relating to well-established sports figures of years past have proved their value while the fame of more recent players may not withstand the test of time.

Baseball Memorabilia
Almost anything connected to this all-American sport is collectible, with baseball cards topping the list. Although age isn't as important as condition, demand, and rarity in pricing cards, pre-1900 examples or those with a mistake are especially desirable. Unfortunately, new graphic techniques make forging "old" cards possible, so be sure to verify a card's authenticity before paying high prices. Look too for team pictures, programs, original photographs of a player out of uniform, pennants, uniforms, and even magazines like *Life* or *Look* with a baseball star on the cover. And remember, items from the early years of a player's career are most valuable.

The Predators
Hunters and fishermen have given us some of the most collectible sporting items. Vintage calendars, posters, and advertising memorabilia depicting sporting scenes can be valuable for their artwork, especially if done by a known artist. Prints, store displays, salesmen's sample catalogs, and counter signs with sporting themes are also of interest. Even old fishing or hunting licenses can be

graphically appealing. ◆ Old fishing poles and reels, fish decoys, lures, and creels also have great decorative potential; those made before 1950 are the most valuable. True fishermen, however, may search out old fly reels or poles simply because of their superior quality. Fish decoys, carved and painted in the likenesses of different fish, are wonderful examples of folk art and are fun to collect because of their visual appeal. Even those made in the '40s and '50s can be expensive if attributed to a known folk artist. For budget-minded collectors, the plastic lures from the '30s are more affordable.

Golf
With the surge of interest in golf over the past few years, enthusiastic players have spurred interest in golf-related collectibles. Everything from balls and clubs to bags, scorecards, posters, programs, tickets, books, trophies, and photos seem to be of interest to someone and the peripheral items are still underpriced. The most obvious flea market finds are old golf clubs, appealing as displays even to nongolfers. Many versions of the rubber-core ball that came into existence in the late 1890s are also collectible. The covers are stamped with hundreds of different designs, such as logos, polka dots, and stars, and occasionally one of the unusual cover patterns used before the standard dimple was adopted in the early 1900s turns up.

Woven fishing creels can be used
as a summer handbag, a bike basket, or wall decor. The choicest are handwoven with leather trim: If the hole in front is on the left rather than the center, it is probably a vintage reproduction like these.

From 1880 to 1890, the trophy
horns that sportsmen took from the buffalo, elk, deer, and moose they hunted were sometimes fashioned into chairs, desks, tables, hat and coat racks, and chandeliers. Piles of horns often show up at flea markets; attach one to a flat piece of wood to fashion a simple coat rack.

Gathering baskets
of all shapes and sizes are lined up in a dealer's booth. They make splendid containers for masses of dried flowers when hung on a wall.

Decoys Hunters may collect firearms, especially any that are stamped Winchester or Remington, or the stuffed mementos of others' successful hunting trips. But decoys are no doubt the most collectible of all hunting items. The rarest can command prices of thousands, but working decoys in less than pristine condition and even some factory-made examples are more affordable. Again, age alone doesn't determine the price; the carving, decoration, and maker are equally important. Oversize heads and twisted head and neck positions generally enhance value. ◆ Floaters were fashioned into every type of duck as well as geese, swans, and even herons and loons. ◆ Because of their size, decoys of larger birds were often made of a canvas-covered wooden frame to keep them light enough to float. "Shadows," flat boards shaped and painted to look like the bird, were another alternative. Since these were easy to make, many simple variations are still around.

A sudden rainstorm created a natural setting for these decoys at Brimfield.

A FISHERMAN'S HIDEAWAY

The old sign above

the door was bought from a couple who had owned a Catskill's fishing camp.

The whimsical lobster

claw lamp, on a cork float with a wooden bobbin doubling as a pull on the chain, is a souvenir of a trip to Maine.

A combination of

slipcovered upholstery and vintage desks and tables allow this fisherman to relax comfortably amid his trophies and gear. A shadowbox showcasing a collection of fishing memorabilia hangs over the sofa.

This collector's treasure

of taxidermy fish, opposite, swims on the barn siding wall over poles and a creel more suitable for a smaller catch.

THE PROPRIETOR OF Ruby Beets and her husband, an avid fisherman, renovated this old barn near the house to provide him with a comfortable retreat in which to work and relax. The weathered barn siding that once sheathed the building was carefully removed, numbered, and reinstalled inside, a perfect background for the handsome collection of fishing paraphernalia. Both useful and decorative, old lures and creels hang from the walls or sit on the desktop, while the sportsman's extensive collection of fishing rods leans casually against the walls. An old watercolor cartoon of a man and wife fishing adds a bit of humor.

Since the owner has always had an affinity for natural things, it was a simple matter to add fish-related items to her flea market wish list. While her husband is "only interested in collecting live fish," the taxidermy fish, known as skin mounts, gleaned from flea markets, estate sales, and antiques dealers, leave little doubt as to his hobby.

GARDEN PICKS

Sandy and John Horvitz were attracted by the sculptural quality of these old garden tools. Enlivened with a new coat of paint, they add a decorative touch to the garden.

A S LONG AS THERE have been gardens there has been a demand for garden furniture, in part because no garden can truly be enjoyed if there isn't a place to sit and take in its beauty. Until the invention of the lawn mower, gardens were the province of the rich and their garden furniture was generally stationary or extremely ornate. But in the mid-1800s when the lawn mower brought lawns to the average person and wealthier Victorians discovered the joys of country homes, a spate of lawn furniture that was strong enough to withstand storms and bright sun yet was

Chris Mead added a glass top to an oversize garden urn to make a handsome table for the entryway of his Bridgehampton house. A folding screen made from a series of charmingly distressed old windows separates the entryway from the living room without blocking the light or the spacious feeling.

easily portable came on the market. Many of the settees and chairs fashioned from wicker, wire, and iron were also charming enough to be used in conservatories and on porches. The rustic styles popular in England were adapted for pieces made of twig, which were perfectly suited to the luxurious but informal camps being built in the Adirondacks. Enhanced by a patina of age, these same chairs, benches, tables, and love seats are now being snapped up to add their undeniable charm to country and city interiors as well as the garden.

In Chris Mead's garden,

a charming old bench beckons invitingly beneath lush cherry blossoms.

CARING FOR OUTDOOR FURNITURE

◆ To remove mildew and stains from natural pine, cedar, and redwood outdoor furniture, scrub with a mild solution of bleach and water. (Test the solution on an inconspicuous spot first, because the bleach may lighten the color of the wood.) Rinse well with clear water, then apply a coat of commercial sealer to protect the wood.

◆ Somewhat distressed painted furniture has a feeling of age and a certain charm, but if you find a piece that is too distressed for your liking, remove the old paint by rubbing with a wire brush, or with a commercial paint remover, depending on how pristine you want it to be. Prime the cleaned piece, then apply two coats of paint. To achieve the flat look of old milk paint inexpensively, color white acrylic paint with powdered pigment and dilute with water to the consistency of heavy cream. (To achieve a peeling effect, see page 160.)

◆ Use fine steel wool or a wire brush to remove rust from metal pieces. Heavily rusted furniture should be sent to a professional sandblaster for restoration. If you leave the metal natural, preserve the finish by spraying with clear lacquer. Otherwise, apply a coat of rust-preventive undercoating, followed by two coats of paint.

◆ Never strip paint from wicker. Stripping makes it more prone to breaking and leaves it rough and hairy. Although it is labor intensive, sanding away old paint is a better option, or use a wire brush to remove flaking paint. Repaint only when necessary. Use several thin coats to avoid flooding any details with excess paint, or save time by spraying carefully.

◆ Experts can repair any damage to wicker pieces, although it may be expensive. To prevent further damage, dust or vacuum wicker occasionally. If a piece is really dirty, take it outside and hose it down with a spray nozzle, then allow it to dry in a shady spot. Wetting it down often eliminates the creaks in unpainted wicker.

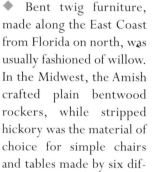

First made in the 1920s, Adirondack chairs have seats fashioned of wood slats, considerably wider at the front and inclining steeply from front to back. A tall back provides comfortable support right to the top of the head and the wide arms are roomy enough to hold a drink. These chairs are still being made by individual craftsmen as well as by commercial manufacturers.

Donna Karan brings the outdoors in, opposite, by painting old garden urns white and filling them with flowers; the coffee table's glass top rests on an old piece of sculpture from a fountain.

INCE THE 1700S Europeans have fashioned furniture and accessories from recognizable parts of trees and bushes. Americans took up this rustic bent in the mid-1800s and quickly made it their own, furnishing resorts and country dwellings with inventive pieces made from whatever the local fields and forests provided most plentifully. ◆ In the Adirondacks, camp guides and local craftsmen were famous for their ability to devise furniture and accessories such as lamps and smoking stands out of local woods, generally combining a polished surface and rough bark in a single piece. Farther north in Maine, pieces were made from both the branches and stumps of hardwood trees as well as twig and birch; birch bark was sometimes applied as decoration. At Appalachian mountain resorts the craftsmen's raw material came from the roots and limbs of laurel and rhododendron, which grew in abundance there; in Florida and the Deep South, they used cypress. ◆ Bent twig furniture, made along the East Coast from Florida on north, was usually fashioned of willow. In the Midwest, the Amish crafted plain bentwood rockers, while stripped hickory was the material of choice for simple chairs and tables made by six different Indiana companies, of which one, the Old Hickory Chair company, is back in business today. ◆ Although interest in this rustic furniture waned in the '30s, in some parts of the country craftsmen never stopped making these charming chairs and tables. In the '70s they reemerged as trendy pieces luring more manufacturers into production. Old pieces are now very collectible.

THE RUSTIC INFLUENCE

these vintage steel chairs
frequently pop up at
flea markets and yard sales,
as do the more ornate
wrought-iron sets from the
'40s and '50s made by
such manufacturers as
Woodward. Reproductions
of earlier pieces abound,
so caveat emptor.

METAL FURNITURE

BECAUSE OF ITS strength, metal has always been a natural choice for garden furniture. In the 19th century, ornate cast-iron pieces were made by the simple process of impressing a carved wood design in sand, then filling the mold with molten iron, which enabled manufacturers to produce intricate designs inexpensively. The chairs, tables, and benches that resulted were influenced by the same trends as indoor furniture, among them gothic, chinoiserie, and rustic. Since this furniture was produced in such abundance, many pieces still exist, but numerous modern copies are also available. Newer pieces are often made of rust-free aluminum, which is considerably lighter, but the detailing of the design is not as sharply defined. ◆ More whimsical pieces were wrought from wire, twisted and turned into fanciful curlicues and stylized spiderwebs, or simply woven like sophisticated chicken wire. Far less sturdy than cast iron, it was also lighter and less expensive. Old chairs, benches, and plant stands still show up at markets, but again, the current popularity of wire has enticed many manufacturers to reproduce a wide variety of pieces. ◆ Some of the most attractive metal garden furniture was produced in France, starting in the last half of the 1800s: chairs and tables with openwork seats and tops, classic chairs constructed of sprung steel, and the well-known button chair whose springy steel seat had more bounce than the best cushion. Their popularity inspired American manufacturers to create their own versions. Much of the original production stopped when World War II created a heavy demand for steel. Before the '40s ended, however, furniture of tubular steel—inexpensive, lightweight, and impervious to weather—came into fashion.

"I like garden furniture," says one of the proprietors of Ruby Beets, "and I use French iron furniture inside, too. I like the idea of inside/ outside." In her garden a mix of bent steel and cast iron surround a small table set under a pergola.

In his country house Chris Mead transforms an old wire plant stand into a handy library.

The painted door
from a Pennsylvania flea
market adds color and interest to the
living room while hiding exposed
pipes in the corner.

Adding to the outdoor
feeling, old toy
garden tools are lined up on
the windowsill like tiny sculptures.

AN ECLECTIC EYE

AT COLLEGE BERNS FRY frequented thrift shops to assemble a trendy wardrobe of Hawaiian shirts, khakis, dress shirts, and even an occasional cashmere sweater. "One day I bought a nice vase," he says, "and then I started looking at home furnishings, too." That was the beginning of his affinity for flea markets and decorating. After moving to New York City, he made frequent sorties to the 26th Street Flea Market to decorate his apartment, eventually realizing he enjoyed going to the flea market more than his job in public relations. He moved to the Hamptons and opened Tag Sale Antiques with a friend, and now going to the flea market is part of the job.

Berns describes his taste as eclectic, finding it more liberating to forage according to whim rather than a prescribed style. Nor does he consider himself a true collector. "What happens," he says, "is I'll find an ashtray in the shape of a leaf at the flea market twice in one day. Then I'll get more and people will give them to me and suddenly I've got a collection."

He is a particular fan of iron and architectural pieces, which he successfully incorporates into a mix of furniture and accessories, much of which would be equally at home in the garden. Sometimes I find broken bits that I really like but wouldn't present at retail," he says, "but I use them in the house." In the living room, for example, urns, stone ornaments, and a tile-topped metal table add decorative accents. Nothing is permanent, however. "I often have pieces for a short time, then pass them on and get something new," says Berns. A price tag on the chest used as a coffee table attests to this constant turnover.

Urns, stone ornaments, balustrades from an old porch railing, and French garden chairs give the dining area, opposite, the feeling of a garden room. An old wire stand doubles as a fruit basket.

In a sunny corner a collection of folk art birdhouses is displayed on a long table. The rattan chairs and twig table contribute to the sense of bringing the outdoors in.

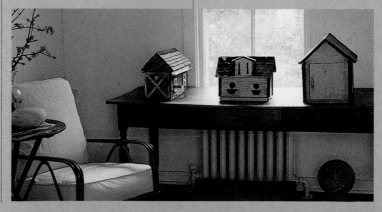

WICKER IS ONE of the most popular categories of indoor/outdoor furniture. Although many people assume wicker refers to the specific material from which the furniture is made, it actually defines the woven construction. With roots that go back to antiquity, wicker has at times been made from cane, willow, reed, rattan, or rush as well as raffia and sea grass. Ancient Egyptian priests sat on reed stools; in the first century Romans carried it with them to England, where local production incorporated the use of willow. By the 16th century, Portuguese traders had added woven rattan furniture from India to their precious cargoes of silks and spices. European craftsmen took heed, began

WICKER

importing rattan, and by the 17th century had appropriated the craft for their own, selling wicker furniture throughout Europe, where woven basket chairs were the most common furniture in peasant houses. By 1750, however, wicker fell out of favor, replaced in public affections by wooden furniture with cushions. ◆ Nearly one hundred years later, shippers were packing their cargoes from Southeast Asia with rattan and discarding it on the docks. A far-seeing Massachusetts manufacturer, Cyrus Wakefield, seized the opportunity to found the American wicker furniture industry. His success propelled others into the business almost immediately, and his most serious competition came from Heywood Brothers. In 1897 the two companies merged, and the hyphenated name was shortened to Heywood-Wakefield Co. in 1921. But from the mid-1800s until the merger, the rivalry encouraged a burst of creativity that resulted in chairs, étagères, tables, settees, and more, all in intricate Victorian rococo designs. Often as well designed as hardwood pieces by Herter and Stickley, wicker was used as country house furniture or for the middle class suburban houses that proliferated after the Civil War. Its popularity was further enhanced by the Victorian obsession with cleanliness and health: Without upholstery it was less likely to attract dust and the openwork designs allowed

Chris Mead has furnished his porch with miscellaneous wicker pieces unified by a coat of paint. A collection of birdhouses decorates the wall.

To turn her upstairs sunporch into a cheery garden room, Christina Redding furnished it with a collection of old wicker chairs, baskets, and a newly painted vintage chest.

air to circulate freely, diminishing unhealthy "stale air" and germs. ◆ By the 1920s wicker pieces were simpler in feeling: The most popular were the "Bar Harbor" designs originated by Joseph P. McHugh of New York. Based on a cross pattern weave, they were very comfortable and widely copied. Cape May inspired another popular pattern. Since wicker lent itself to the spare feeling of Arts and Crafts design as well as it had to the earlier curlicues, Gustav Stickley designed some simple wicker pieces and there were even a few Art Deco pieces painted or lacquered in the distinctive color schemes of that era. America's romance with wicker ended in the '30s, however, with the arrival of sleeker Art Deco- and Bauhaus-inspired designs. ◆ In the '70s wicker furniture recaptured the public's fancy and manufacturers were quick to make new pieces to satisfy the demand. Much of this new wicker is handcrafted in Asia and does not compare in either design or quality with earlier pieces, so flea market wicker is often the best. Since Victorian wicker was frequently custom-made, however, you should try a chair on for size before buying. ◆ A few facts can help you date wicker furniture. Victorian pieces were generally made of narrower cane that was easier to fashion into the curlicues of the day. Pieces made after 1900 tend to be more loosely woven with thicker cane shaped into rectilinear forms. Generally speaking, the older the wicker, the heavier it will be. The finish on a wicker piece can also help date it. In the last half of the 1800s, most pieces were left natural except for a clear finish; a few were stained dark green or a wood hue. At the turn of the century, painted wicker became more popular, making the naturally weather-resistant pieces even more practical for outdoor use. ◆ Whether wicker is old or new, always check the frame carefully before buying, because although experts can repair damage to the reeds rather easily, repairing a frame is a major job. Also try to determine if the woven material is still supple. Dried, brittle material may snap if the piece will have to bear weight.

In Rawley Sorman's living room, a handsomely shaped green wicker sofa and the white wicker chairs are cushioned with a variety of old fabrics found on her outings. Luckily for Rawley, when she finds a piece in need of repair, her husband volunteers.

With a stroke of creativity native to all good flea market sleuths, Thomas Rosamilia has transformed a splint bassinet into a fern-filled plant stand. An old watering can is another flea market find.

RADITIONAL garden statuary and urns are also common flea market offerings, but unexpected architectural remnants, bits of folk art, and more imaginative finds like an old washtub that can be turned into a planter or set on a stump to become a birdbath also make interesting garden decorations. Like old watering cans and tools, they stamp a garden with their owner's personality, and they double as decorative accessories. And don't forget that many items originally intended for use in the garden only are even more intriguing out of context indoors. In the hands of creative flea marketers, watering cans and birdhouses turn up as lamps; urns are filled with dried flowers; and gates are hung as art. The trick is to look at garden accessories and ornaments with an open mind—even if you don't have a garden.

DECORATIVE ELEMENTS

In Malibu, Andrea Dern adapts an old plant stand for displaying her collection of colorful vintage watering cans.

A COUNTRY DEALER

KATHY SHORR developed her collector's eye as a documentary photographer. Even though her work had been successfully published and exhibited both here and in Europe, after a boyfriend took her on a trip to his native Kentucky to buy some furniture she was transformed into an antiques dealer. She brought a trove of wonderful old country pieces she discovered there back to New York and within three weeks had sold everything to stores in Brooklyn and SoHo for a handsome profit. Some well-placed publicity and a lot of work have since combined to turn her into a well-known dealer of country furniture with a long list of private clients, many of whom she met when she had a space at New York's 26th Street Flea Market.

Kathy spends most weeks out hunting for the furniture, folk art, paintings, and prints that she sells by appointment from her downtown Manhattan loft or at the occasional show. "I'm constantly scrambling," she says, "but I only buy what I like. It's my style, and it gives someone

else a way to go. Generally I opt for things with character, something someone's made for whatever function for their own use." Old frames are another favorite that allow her to do all her own framing.

Whether it's a trip to the nearby 26th Street Flea Market, a big show in Connecticut, or an auction in Maryland, Kathy Shorr looks for objects that have a tactile quality and some color. "I like to transform old pieces," she says.

The old bamboo plant stand in Kathy Shorr's hall found a second life as a handsome little table after she added a glass top. Other pieces, like the old kitchen chair, are admired for their character: The various layers of paint reveal the color preferences of previous owners.

In the living room, shutters in two shades of green have been transformed into a screen that acts as a room divider, providing more wall space to show off her acquisitions. Paintings and prints that need framing are treated to a selection from her flea market collection. The simple painted table and chair, probably from someone's kitchen, show endearing signs of use.

MAKING A SCREEN

Kathy Shorr used three old pine tree shutters

to create a folding screen for her bedroom. Depending on the size needed, such screens can be assembled from as few as two shutters or from many.

IT'S A SIMPLE MATTER TO MAKE a screen out of several old matching shutters. All it takes is a bit of patience and a few supplies from the local lumberyard. If a set of old shutters proves elusive, buy some new ones and create a vintage feeling by using the flaking paint techniques on page 160.

1. If you want feet on the screen, measure one-sixth of the way in from each side on the bottom of each shutter. Screw in knobs or glue feet in place; hold firmly in place with a vise or string until they are thoroughly dry. (If you expect to move the screen frequently, secure the feet with finishing nails after the glue is dry.)

2. Lay the 3 shutters side by side on the ground. Carefully measure and mark the center of each adjoining side. This will be where the center hinge goes. Then measure and mark one-third of the way from the top to the center. Repeat, measuring from the bottom. This will determine the placement of the remaining hinges.

3. Center a hinge on the center mark between 2 shutters. Attach one side; then, making sure the shutters are aligned exactly, attach the second side. Repeat with the top and bottom hinges. Join the third shutter in the same way.

the
PAPER
CHASE

PAPER COLLECTIBLES range from postcards and old labels for as little as a dollar or two to rare posters, fine prints, and photographs. Other readily available paper collectibles inspiring someone somewhere to start a collection include matchbooks, which are gaining in popularity as smoking declines; ticket stubs from theaters or sporting events; colorful seed packets; beer bottle labels; vintage paper dolls; even old stock market certificates and report cards.

Pages from an old artist's sketchbook are tacked casually on the wall of Ellen O'Neill's dining room, where the look of the graphite and faded yellow paper combines pleasingly with the distressed walls.

I NEXPENSIVE bits of paper, letters, prints, labels, books, pamphlets, postcards, and catalogs abound at flea markets, and sometimes entire shows are devoted to these small bits of paper known as ephemera. As the name suggests, these paper goods were not designed to have lasting value; however, they now offer us an interesting and often decorative glimpse of history, and may in fact have appreciated a great deal in value. Many of these items can complement a broader collection; for example, baseball cards are sought after by many sports enthusiasts. Some of the more popular areas are highlighted below.

Postcards

Postcards appeal to collectors because they are plentiful and depict a broad range of subjects. The first commercial cards in the United States, printed in 1892 to commemorate the Columbian Exposition, started a fervor of postcard collecting that lasted until World War I and has resurfaced again today. ◆ Serious collectors prefer cards printed before the turn of the century; a postmark often helps date the card. Art Nouveau, well-known artists, interiors, and holiday greetings are among the most desirable subjects, along with geographical areas, especially hometowns; photographs of people; patriotic or political subjects; historical events; transportation; or black subjects. A collection of cards from less coveted fields like flowers can still be assembled inexpensively. ◆ Keep your collection in an album or frame it for display. Use less valuable cards to decorate screens, boxes, and other items, and blank cards to write notes to your friends.

Posters

From the 1880s until after the turn of the century, spectacular posters delivering an advertising message proliferated all through Europe and the United States, many of them created by such important artists as Toulouse-Lautrec, Aubrey Beardsley, and Maxfield Parrish. These, along with some fine examples from later dates, especially from the Art Deco era, are now known

Vintage postcards are generally offered in neatly cataloged boxes, but a pile tossed casually on a table might offer an interesting find to a collector patient enough to sort through it.

EPHEMERA

Create a spot to display postcards by refurbishing an old screen with vintage fabric, then tacking on ribbon pulled taut enough to hold the cards in place.

Even contemporary posters, whether political or musical, can be a collectible.

CARING FOR FINE PAPER ITEMS

◆ Store paper items in a cool, dry place. Heat and humidity encourage mold. If books or papers develop mold, use a camel hair brush to whisk it off, then place the object in the sun for one hour.

◆ Never trim the edges of a print unless badly damaged. Leave any descriptive text at the bottom.

◆ To repair small tears in paper, tease the edges together with a needle, then apply a small amount of wheat paste. Put a piece of blotter on both sides of the tear and press the paper between two weights. Change the blotter after five minutes, and then again after another five minutes. Replace the blotter with waxed paper and leave between the weights overnight.

◆ Layer prints and pictures between sheets of acid-free tissue or sleeves and store in acid-free folders or envelopes (available at art supply stores). Mat valuable pieces before storing. Though it's best to store artwork flat, if you want to keep prints or posters in a tube, put acid-free tissue on the face before rolling and never roll them tighter than 3 inches.

◆ Mount prints or photos only if poor condition mandates it. Use wet mounting on items that will be affected by heat; dry mounting for poor-quality paper.

◆ If the paper is dirty, dusty, or greasy, brush off surface dirt with a soft brush, then gently clean it with dry eraser powder, or use an art gum eraser on stronger paper. The insides of a moist slice of bread, rolled into a soft ball, can be an effective substitute for an eraser and can also be used on paintings.

◆ Stains from cellophane tape can be removed by carefully applying a mixture of one part acetone, three parts alcohol, and three parts toluene, a solvent.

◆ When appropriate, use a frame to protect paper from dust and grime. Mats should be acid free. Seal the back completely to guard against dust and bugs. Moisture is less likely to condense behind Plexiglas than glass. UF-3 Plexiglas, slightly tinted to deflect ultraviolet light, helps prevent fading and deterioration from bright sun.

◆ Do not hang pictures above a radiator, heat duct, or fireplace.

◆ Tungsten light is easier on photographs than fluorescent or intense halogen light.

◆ Excessive heat curls and cracks photographs; dampness encourages mildew or may cause them to stick together. To restore crumpled or stuck photographs, lay them facedown on polyester interfacing on a damp blotter. Press with a warm iron. The moist heat released through the interfacing will thin the emulsion so the pictures come unstuck and help smooth the paper.

◆ Don't keep valuable photos in a magnetic album and never glue them directly to a page; use photo corners instead.

◆ To remove foxing from a black-and-white print, place it on a piece of glass slightly larger than the print. Fill a nonmetallic tub with a mixture of one tablespoon of bleach to two quarts of water and submerge the glass-backed print. Leave it until the spots have faded or disappeared. Carefully remove the glass with the print and empty the tub. Return the print and glass to the tub and run cool water over the print for twice as long as it soaked in the bleach solution. Remove it once again and flip the print onto a large desk blotter. Carefully remove the glass, put a second blotter on top of the print, and cover with the glass to prevent curling as it dries.

◆ When dusting the top of a book, be sure to dust away from the spine. Keep the book and jacket in prime condition with a clear acetate cover.

◆ Never glue, stitch, or tape an old book. If valuable, take it to a professional restorer. Otherwise, keep it in an acid-free box.

◆ Clean morocco or calf leather-bound books by applying cream saddle soap to the leather with a soft cloth. Keep the soap away from any gold lettering and the paper. Wipe clean with a cloth. To keep the leather supple, wipe with a cotton ball dipped in leather dressing or lanolin and then squeezed as dry as possible. After it is dry, wipe again with a clean cotton ball.

as fine art posters, and although expensive remain good investments. ◆ Collecting isn't limited to art posters, however. Old show and movie posters can be interesting, too, and for purely decorative possibilities, look for the old travel posters once used to romance customers. Prices are determined by good graphics, the artist, the subject, and, above all, the condition.

Labels

Fruit crate and cigar labels boasting colorful, eye-catching images are decorative and inexpensive. Crate labels were developed for identification and advertising purposes in the late 1800s, and over the years more than ten thousand designs featuring the cowboys, Indians, and the bounty of the American West were created. By the 1920s labels were more brand oriented and primarily graphic. When preprinted cardboard cartons made labels redundant, the many unused examples left in the warehouses found their way to flea markets and collectors. ◆ Luggage labels can still be had for a song. From the '20s to the '50s, airlines, hotels, and transatlantic liners provided colorful labels to their customers, for whom they were a status symbol.

Emelie Tolley's collection of old French syrup and liqueur labels turns a collection of bottled libations into a decorative display.

Travel labels are among the most interesting and colorful of those offered for sale. The best depict exotic designs or use Art Deco graphics.

Suitcases are a hot collectible, especially when covered with old travel labels that convey a sense of romance and adventure. They provide decorative storage or can be stacked to serve as a low chairside table.

A VISUAL APPROACH

As a child in Massachusetts, John Derian collected rocks, shells, and other found objects, and at an early age headed to the Brimfield flea market with his older sister. "Even then I was interested in changing my environment," he says. "Now I go to the flea market to find treasures. Pieces sort of speak to me." These treasures really give him joy, especially when he rearranges the room to fit them in, a pastime he finds very stimulating. More visual than verbal, John uses objects to express himself to others and to create a space that's very soothing to him and his friends.

Rather than decorate in the usual sense, John collects furniture and objects that appeal to his aesthetics. "Anyone can go to Bloomingdale's," observes John, "but things at the flea market are more special." Always looking for quirky pieces, John, now a resident of New York City, tries to get to the 26th Street Flea Market early before others find that something special he might want. "Although I never go searching for one particular

item, I generally make a quick run-through looking for big pieces, then go back and look for smalls," he says. Among the smaller objects he seeks are handwritten and printed pages, which he incorporates into the découpage plates, lamps, mirrors, and cachepots he creates for stores across the country as well as in Europe and South America.

Interacting with the dealers is another pleasant part of flea market shopping. "Generally the dealers are nice," he says. "And there's a sense of connection because you like something they've found. When you chat with the dealer about the age, character, and history of a piece it becomes a social event for you both."

Although the flea market treasures

may be distressed, John Derian's living room has a feeling of elegance. Once a fan of stacking objects, he now gives things more space so each piece has room to breathe. The couch, covered in slightly worn silk damask, was found at a flea market in Salem, Massachusetts. The hand-painted paper screen is a present from a friend who knew John liked distressed pieces.

Some of the interesting old books

John has found are kept on a bookcase in the hall for ready reference.

Tracy Gill and
Simeon Lagodich's
store of old books shares
space with favorite architectural remnants and other
treasured objects in the
specially built shelves of
their Tribeca loft.

Vintage
magazines yield
collectible advertisements,
illustrations, or a glimpse of
life in another time.

Old books range
from "fillers"
for your shelves to out-of-
print tomes filled with
fascinating information
and beautiful old plates.

READING MATTER

B OOKS ARE AMONG the most rewarding of paper collectibles. While rare old editions are for the serious collector only, at more modest prices you can often find lovely and informative old volumes on cooking, gardening, decorating, history, and almost any other subject, many with handsome plates. Some are so beautifully bound you may be tempted to buy them for the case alone. And although they may be classified as advertising, little cookbooks, once used as premiums for flours or even patent medicines, can be found for a few dollars and can give a quick insight into what people were eating earlier in this century. Catalogs, especially seed catalogs containing color prints, are also enticing. ◆ Many collectors seek out magazines from the last part of the 19th century up to the present. Comic strips, first published just before the turn of the century, and comic books from the '30s until today are runaway best-sellers. Among the most popular are Marvel and Action comics. Movie magazines, old fashion magazines, and *National Geographics* are also very collectible—and almost any magazine might be useful to someone if it contains interesting advertisements or work by a well-known author or illustrator, as did some *Harper's Weekly* magazines from the 1860s.

A LITERARY HALLWAY

JOHN DERIAN buys lots of old books for the prints they contain, which he uses in his découpage projects. Rather than recycle the remaining pages through regular channels, he used them to wallpaper his hallway, a fitting choice since his designs frequently include bits of manuscript. Because John likes a no-color look, he used the lightest pages. The same technique can also be used to cover a screen, a trunk, or a box. You might even want to try it on a table or chest of drawers.

MATERIALS

Books of 6 varying sizes
White glue thinned with water
Clean, dry rags
Straightedge razor blades or
X-Acto knife
Nonyellowing matte finish
water-soluble polyurethane
(optional)

1. Place the pages in separate stacks according to size. The different sizes will be applied randomly, overlapping for a better fit and a more pleasing pattern.

2. Select a page, place it on the work surface, and brush the thinned white glue over the back. (To make the process quicker and easier, lay out 6 separate work spaces the same sizes as the pages. This allows you to select whichever size page you need and set it face-down in its own space to avoid getting glue on the face.)

3. Starting at one corner at the top of the wall, apply the page to the wall and pat it firmly in place with a dry rag. Work your way across the wall in rows. When pages must be trimmed around a door or window, press in place, then cut away overhang with a sharp razor.

4. If desired, apply a coat of polyurethane to protect the surface after the glue has completely dried.

In John Derian's hallway, pages from old books, recycled as wallpaper, add pale color and a subtle sense of pattern.

A group of bird prints turns a pair of old windows into two attractive screens. Attach a simple footed stand to stabilize them; add a decorative piece of woodwork to finish the tops. You can also use color copies of your favorite prints made to size.

PRINTS

P RINTS OF FLOWERS, animals, scenes, or political events have always been a popular and an inexpensive way of enjoying the work of a well-known artist. During the 1700s and 1800s they were actually used to record important events and botanical knowledge as well as to disseminate knowledge about decoration and fashion. After the Civil War, photographs became the preferred method of documentation. ◆ Prints may be produced from woodcuts, engravings, etchings, mezzotints, lithographs, or chromolithographs. Early illustrations in newspapers, posters and advertising labels for boxes and crates, magazine covers, and sheet music were often woodcuts. However, the majority of inexpensive vintage color items will be chromoliths, the only method for mass-producing color before four-color presses were invented. ◆ There are a few ways to establish which method was used. Engravings and etchings are often signed, dated,

Hand-colored for greater appeal, these old botanical prints are almost modern in their graphic simplicity.

Even inexpensive floral prints make

a strong statement when hung en masse, as they are in John Derian's shop. The prints are framed between glass and cardboard anchored with plate hangers, a quick and economical solution to multiple framing jobs.

and numbered, while lithographs will have the name of the company who produced them along with the line "entered according to the act of Congress in the year ———." Currier and Ives were among the best known of the lithographers: others were Sarony, Major and Knapp, Kurz, and Allison, while some of the major artists were Wallace Nutting, Maxfield Parrish, and Icart. Many old lithos have been reproduced, but with the help of a magnifying glass you can tell if you have an original: A lithograph is composed of fine lines, while a photographic copy will be made up of tiny dots. As you become more knowledgeable, you'll see the difference in the look and smell of old paper, which is generally heavy and porous, while new paper has a slight sheen. ◆ Even inexpensive reproduction prints, although they will probably never be of great value, can be decorative when hung in a large grouping, applied to the wall to create an English "Print Room," or cut apart to découpage a lamp, screen, or other object.

Seed packets are still reasonably

priced because many unused packets were left in warehouses when companies went out of business. Such pristine specimens are handsome when framed.

PAPER COLLECTIBLES

◆ Items that are amusing or have historical significance.

◆ Political subjects, cars, airplanes, balloons, western subjects, and well-known artists such as Wallace Nutting or Maxfield Parrish. Religious and sentimental subjects are less desirable.

◆ Photographs of 19th- or early-20th-century celebrities or transportation; fashion photos by well-known photographers; American Indian subjects; people in work clothing, especially from defunct occupations; historical landmarks and events. Printed and signed photos are most valuable. Watch out for reprints.

◆ Good design and beauty. They are as important as price.

◆ Books in good condition with a dust cover and no damaged or missing pages. In some cases, a first edition or an author's signature also increases the value.

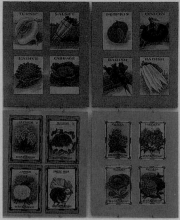

Tape, paste, or glue

Creases, tears, and dirt on the surface

Gouges or erasures

Off-register or poor-quality printing

Worn corners or trimmed images

Signs of bleaching (a chalky surface)

Foxing (brown spots that can only be partially removed)

Note: Some people think a small amount of foxing adds a charming patina of age.

Mary Baltz used frames from yard sales and flea markets for this gallery of family photos in the stairwell. Although she wanted her daughter to live with the old photographs as she grew up, she also wanted to protect them from bright sunlight. The solution: Photocopies are on display; the fragile originals are stored safely away.

PHOTOGRAPHS

PHOTOGRAPHS ARE AN up-and-coming area, too, and although photographic prints by Ansel Adams and other pioneers are extremely expensive, scouring flea markets will turn up some excellent examples of the photographer's art produced by long-forgotten people with an unheralded talent. A collection based on subject or type, even very simply framed, becomes a striking graphic display. And a group of simple snapshots can be an endearing window into the daily lives of the subjects and the times. ◆ Although daguerreotypes (1839 to 1860) and tintypes (1856 to 1900) can be found, paper-printed photos abound at flea markets. Among the most collectible are cartes de visite and cabinet cards, both dating from the last half of the 19th century. The former were portraits mounted on a $2\frac{1}{2} \times 4$-inch card; the latter were slightly larger ($4\frac{1}{2} \times 6\frac{1}{2}$ inches) and often of groups of people. Collectible in their own time, they were kept in special albums, which occasionally are found intact. Stereotypes, produced from 1851 into the 1930s, are also an amusing collectible. These double images mounted on cardboard produced a 3-D effect when viewed through a special viewer called a stereopticon.

OVERLEAF:

Bobby Bant uses her collections

to create vignettes throughout her Florida house. Old family photos in flea market frames are displayed on a table created from simple pedestals as well as on the wall. Unrelated sports collectibles add interest to the display.

SHADES OF SUMMER

ALEX SIGMON combines his artist's eye, a talent for display, and old photos and keys collected on flea market jaunts to create one-of-a-kind lamps for Hunters & Collectors, the antiques store he owns with partner Alexander Jakowec on eastern Long Island. Starting with an old lamp shade from the flea market, he refurbishes it with a covering of raffia, then ties on keys and tucks in old photos.

MATERIALS

Working lamp with distressed wire-framed shade
Raffia
Old keys
Raffia cloth or parchment
Old photos

1. Strip the lamp shade down to the wire frame. Tie the end of a piece of raffia to the top rim; wrap it completely, adding new strands as needed, then tie it off. Repeat on the bottom rim.

2. Tie another piece of raffia to one of the ribs abutting the top rim. Wrap the raffia around the next rib and continue around, tying in another piece of raffia when necessary, until the shade is covered. As you wrap the raffia around the ribs, push it tightly against the preceeding strand so the wire is completely covered. The knots where the pieces are added are part of the charm.

3. Use raffia to tie keys to the ribs, spacing them randomly.

4. Cut pieces of raffia cloth or parchment approximately the same size as the space between the ribs. Weave the cloth under the strands of raffia from the inside of the shade, allowing about 1 inch between strands. This spacing can be adjusted to please the eye according to the size of the shade.

5. Tuck the photos into the raffia on the right side of the shade in a pleasing pattern.

Snapshots of yesteryear's vacations

and keys to long-forgotten locks, all gathered at yard sales and flea markets, find new life on a hand-crafted lampshade.

WALL DECOR

ALTHOUGH WALLS ARE intentionally left bare in some splendidly designed contemporary spaces, most of us feel the need to break the monotony. Seasoned flea market goers know that a little searching will turn up attractive and affordable alternatives to inexpensive posters and reproductions, providing them with something both real and old to grace their walls. Paintings, prints, drawings, and photographs are obvious solutions, but mirrors also fill bare space handsomely and their reflective surfaces can add a feeling of space. Wall sconces serve a practical purpose in a decorative way. Even favorite objects

Chris Mead always keeps an eye out for paintings, especially landscapes, flowers, and still lifes of food. As his collection grew, he virtually papered the walls of his den with his acquisitions.

such as a piece of old needlework, pages of pressed leaves and flowers from an old botanical study, and fans are framed and hung. And since prices remain reasonable on many of these items, it's possible to create stunning groupings without breaking the bank. ◆ As more and more people shop at flea markets and learn to rely on their own decorative sense, they are displaying their finds with greater imagination, and the scope of wall decor has expanded to include many nontraditional objects, framed or not. Old painted doors, gates, bits of lace, and empty frames are a few of the treasures turning up on collectors' walls, and when like objects are grouped together, they make an even bigger impression. ◆ If one of your collections isn't being shown to its full potential, consider hanging it on the wall. Although we traditionally hang pictures in the main living areas, a barbershop collection might be shown to advantage in a bathroom, hats or sporting goods might enliven a hallway, or watering cans might brighten a porch.

Old frames are frequently

great bargains. Even if you don't have paintings in need of framing, they can be filled with mirrors or even hang empty on a wall if they are decorative enough.

The striking metal sculpture that

hangs in Alex Exarchos's New York apartment began life as the back of a neon sign in a gas station.

Using her artist's eye, Bobby Bant

has amassed collections in many different areas, all of which blend harmoniously with the beautiful objects she creates herself. Here, an empty frame, miniature bull's-eye mirror, and an old clock face hang over a table holding a pique assiette vase and hand-painted china from her own studio. Under the table are examples from her collections of footstools, leatherbound books, and loving cups.

O BJECTS OF BEAUTY and interest in themselves, traditional frames were ignored during much of the second half of this century because contemporary artists believed they distracted from the work itself. That's one reason frames show up in such abundance at flea markets, where for the past ten years artists and other astute collectors have been snapping them up as much for their decorative qualities as their utilitarian ones. In 1990 the Metropolitan Museum of Art even installed a permanent collection of antique American frames. ◆ Whether it's a gilded beauty or an amusing tramp art piece, sooner or later you'll find a frame that speaks to you.

FRAMES

It may come complete with an old painting or photo, but unless it's a valuable work or one that especially appeals to you, you can feel free to replace it with artwork of your choosing. Don't let size be a deterrent; if it's a relatively close fit, adding a mat could solve the problem, and a major difference in size can often be overcome by sending the frame to a professional to be recut. Don't worry if you don't have an immediate need for a frame you love; eventually it is bound to prove useful. Until it does, display the empty frame on the wall and enjoy its inherent beauty and charm.

Artist Hunt
Slonem decorates

the wall of his bedroom with
a collection of small paintings
handsomely framed in flea
market purchases. The gothic
chair is one of many he's
acquired from flea markets
and antiques dealers,
and the ceiling is home to a
collection of mercury witches'
balls suspended from
colorful velvet ropes.

Gold frames

in good condition but with
the warming patina of wear
are quickly snapped up by
flea market buffs.

Bobby Bant, a multifaceted artist, searches flea markets in her native Florida and as far away as Brimfield, Massachusetts, for frames. Although she uses some for her own work, an ever-changing grouping is displayed in an armoire or hung on a wall empty so she can admire their intrinsic decorative features.

A matching pair of framed artworks captures the eye of a buyer who may be more interested in the frames than their contents.

FRAME SAVVY

A PASSION FOR frames is one of the things that brought Tracy Gill and Simeon Lagodich together. Their Tribeca loft is a fantasy of gilded shapes from 19th- and early-20th-century frame makers hanging one inside the other on every available wall of the living area.

Both are artists: Simeon concentrates on large American realist landscapes, while Tracy experiments with shades of gold in small paintings and objects such as elaborate "Turkish" floor cloths. In the 1980s Simeon began searching for frames for his paintings at flea markets, but soon the pair found themselves

Excellent craftsmanship has earned Tracy Gill

and Simeon Lagodich a well-deserved reputation as experts on American frames and restoration that has led to work with museums and serious private collectors. Many of their flea market finds are displayed in their loft.

buying more frames than they could use and began selling the extras to other artists, photographers, and decorators. Now they have a thriving business.

As dawn breaks on most Saturday mornings, Tracy and Simeon are on their way to one or more flea markets to look for frames of every size and type. While they are known for unearthing beautifully crafted and gilded frames, they also keep a watchful eye out for the miniframes and quirky folk art pieces that make up their respective personal collections. "We tend to buy everything," Tracy says. "Frames are the best single bargain in the market now," adds Simeon. "They're undervalued, but that's changing." While not every jaunt turns up good buys, Simeon likens the exhilaration of a good day to winning at the gaming tables in Atlantic City.

Although many of the less serious decorative frames are offered to clients in their original state, more important gilded painting frames in period styles from the 19th and early 20th centuries are

carefully restored and regilded. "These frames were valuable when they were made," says Simeon, "and good-quality examples have increased in value."

Since there is little literature on the subject, these experts suggest you learn about frames by talking with dealers and watching what sells first thing in the morning. Even eavesdropping on conversations can yield important information. And if you see a frame that's priced beyond your limits, Simeon suggests making a friendly offer to the seller and returning at the end of the day. "He may not have had any nibbles and want out," he says.

Simeon cautions buyers of quality frames to examine them closely for any signs of poor restoration such as paint, plaster, or gum. "There is always problematical merchandise at flea markets," he says, "and you can be sure that if a frame is painted, it's for a reason. Restoring a badly damaged piece can cost up to four times the price of the frame."

Tracy and Simeon are both knowledgeable gilders; he is self-taught, she has taken courses. They approach their work with the dedication of old-time craftsmen, using only the traditional painstaking and time-consuming methods of water gilding rather than the quicker shortcuts possible with synthetic materials. The frames are then rubbed for hours to give them just the right patina.

Since Tracy Gill likes to do small paintings, collecting small frames seemed logical. "I think of them as pieces of jewelry, and they take less room," she says. "They're really like the big frames shrunk down, so it's a way to have room for an example of every style."

SIMPLE GILDING

Although Tracy Gill and Simeon Lagodich would never use this quick gilding method on their period frames, it can be an effective way to disguise small imperfections on an old wood frame, small decorative objects, or furniture details. Gold leaf, silver leaf, or less expensive Dutch metal leaf comes in books of 25 3 × 3-inch sheets; each book will cover a *smooth* 11 × 14-inch surface.

MATERIALS

*0 and 000 grade steel wool
and sand paper
Tack cloth
Mineral spirits
Premixed polymer gesso
Red tinting color
White shellac
Gold size
Flat brushes for painting,
one soft and one semi-stiff
Enough gold or metallic leaf
to cover the surface
Clear varnish
Burnt umber artist's oil paint
Butcher's wax*

1. Remove all traces of paint or previous finishes from the object, then sand with 0 Grade steel wool until very smooth. Wipe with a tack cloth to remove any dust particles; then rub with a lint-free rag dampened with mineral spirits.

2. Tint the gesso with the red tinting color, then brush on 3 to 4 thin coats, allowing 2 hours between coats, and a little longer after the final coat. When the gesso is completely dry, sand it lightly with fine sandpaper, and rub with the tack cloth.

3. To seal the gesso, combine 2 parts shellac to 1 part mineral spirits. Apply 2 coats. When this is completely dry, brush on a coat of gold size.

4. When the gold size feels tacky enough to hold the leaf (it should register a fingerprint), pick up a sheet of gold leaf by its backing and place it face-down on the prepared surface. Be careful: the leaf is very fragile. Using a fingertip or the semi-stiff brush, apply pressure until the sheet is firmly adhered all over, then remove the backing. Repeat until the frame is completely covered, overlapping the sheets slightly. Remove any excess gold leaf with a soft brush. Dry for at least 12 hours.

5. To give the frame an aged patina, rub the frame down with 000 steel wool, allowing a little of the gesso to show through.

6. Brush with a coat of clear varnish thinned with mineral spirits and barely tinted with burnt umber. Allow to dry for 24 hours. Rub down with the steel wood again, and apply a second coat of varnish.

7. To protect the frame, rub with a thin layer of wax.

F LEA MARKETS AND thrift shops prove fertile grounds for collectors of paintings. Not too long ago, numerous inexpensive paintings by aspiring but unsuccessful artists or ladies who painted for pleasure dotted flea market stalls, but a sudden interest in these naive works has made them scarcer and more expensive. Condition, subject, and the artist's skill all help to determine a work's price. Less-than-mint-condition works are more affordable, and many collectors feel a bit of wear contributes a sense of history to their considerable charm. An attractive frame generally adds to the price and in some cases may even be worth more than the painting. Don't hesitate to buy unframed oil paintings if they are on boards or stretched canvas; they can be hung as is, or you can try to find an old frame at the next market. Watercolors, on the other hand, require the protection and backing of a frame, and unmounted pieces may be in poor condition. ◆ If you collect paintings of a particular subject, hang them in groups: Collections make even lesser paintings look better and create greater impact. The choices include landscapes, garden scenes, flowers of every sort, winter scenes, seascapes, animals, and still lifes of food. Small paintings of any subject are generally less expensive but can be used effectively as part of a tabletop display or grouped together on the wall. ◆ Look also for yard-long paintings. These long, narrow canvases became popular during the Victorian era as artists painted dogs, cats, women, Indians, pansies, roses, and other subjects

This Long Island antiques dealer,

with a particular talent for uncovering appealing paintings for her shop, Ruby Beets, concentrates on florals and portraits. Paintings are often rotated between the shop and her house, where they may be stacked casually against the wall. The chair has been slipcovered with a recycled floral print.

At Brimfield,

a stylish painted lady reclines in a chair while awaiting a buyer.

PAINTINGS AND DRAWINGS

by the yard. They turn up now and then (as do prints of the same genre), and the unexpected shape and history make them especially appealing. ◆

Paint-by-numbers art from the 1940s and '50s is also attracting interest and is still widely available. Although a few of these paintings were done in the '30s, the craze really began in the late '40s, when Max Klein, the owner of a paint store, and Dan Robbins, an artist, had the self-serving idea of producing kits. At the height of their popularity in the early '50s, fifty thousand kits a day were sold, and by 1954 a total of twelve million had found their way into the hands of would-be artists. Their legacy is now collectible. ◆

Serious art collectors approach drawings as a less expensive way to own the work of a well-known artist, but drawings that turn up at flea markets more often represent unheralded talent or charming naïveté. With patience it's possible to sort through portfolios of drawings, some old, some done more recently by students, and come up with a reputable collection. Since this is not investment spending, the sole criterion is that the drawing appeal to you.

Once used to lure customers in a diner, this graphically pleasing old sign now decorates a living room wall.

The co-proprietor of Ruby Beets hangs a gallery of "friends" culled from flea markets and antiques stores in the hallway of her Long Island home.

In her living room, a group of pressed ferns from a Victorian lady's album is framed with the thinnest glass and galley clips for a more contemporary look.

CARING FOR PAINTINGS

◆ Try to keep paintings in an environment with relatively stable humidity and temperature and avoid exposing them to direct sunlight, bright daylight, fluorescent lights, or blasts of heat from a radiator or air duct. If you illuminate a painting, keep incandescent bulbs far enough away to prevent their heat from affecting it.

◆ Never hang a treasured painting in the bathroom: There's too much moisture.

◆ Dust paintings twice yearly with a soft camel hair artist's brush. A feather duster can loosen and remove flakings of paint.

◆ If a painting is in good shape with no flaking paint, you can clean some of the surface dirt by carefully rolling a wad of soft bread (no crusts) over the surface. More serious cleaning––or the cleaning of a fragile or very costly painting––should be left to experts.

◆ If some of the finish has flaked off your gold leaf frame, try a test patch of burnt sienna watercolor. If it blends in with the underlying tone of the frame, use a small paintbrush to touch up the bare spot.

◆ Tip: If you put a hole in a white wall, then change your mind about the placement of a painting, use white toothpaste to do a cosmetic touch-up and hide the hole.

John Derian created this vignette of interesting objects for his antiques store. The handsome wall covering is a hand-painted backdrop from a touring theater troupe. The unfilled frame, a decoration in itself, rests on an old fireplace tool stand instead of the more expected easel.

Alex Exarchos uncovered this pair of distinctive Art Deco prints at a New York City flea market. When he first saw them, they were encased in ugly turquoise frames; reframed, their true artistic worth is obvious.

An equestrian theme unifies the flea market paintings and photographs grouped in a corner of the cottage, opposite, owned by one of the proprietors of Ruby Beets.

The distressed elegance of an old dresser mirror fits seamlessly into this Long Island country bathroom.

MIRRORS

A collection of outstanding mirrors is on display at an outdoor house-and-garden show near Amsterdam.

ALTHOUGH THE EARLIEST mirrors were of polished metal, the Romans occasionally fashioned small mirrors of lead-backed glass. By the 15th century, German glassblowers had discovered how to make convex mirrors whose size and shape depended on the blown glass bubble, and by 1500 Venetian glassblowers had developed the technology to produce large, flat mercury-backed mirrors. These Venetian mirrors became popular throughout Europe until, in the 17th century, a new French technique made larger, even-surfaced mirrors possible. Since then mirrors have become a major decorative accent, their shapes and frames complementing the furniture style of the times. As a result, it's possible to find examples framed in extraordinarily ornate frames as well as in the plainest pine. ◆ A trip to the flea market will expand your options even further. Look for architecturally interesting windows or doors and fill the panes with mirrors; cut an opening in a decorative piece of tin ceiling tile; fashion a piece of antique molding into a frame; or take a discarded mirror from a dresser or armoire and recycle it as a wall mirror. Large mirrors can be placed against the wall as well as hung; small mirrors can be grouped together for added impact. All will add sparkle, light, and space to a room. ◆ If you come upon an antique mirror, you may find that the mercury backing has developed spots. These are caused by moisture trapped behind the wooden backing. Although many people consider this mottled appearance charming and a sign of natural aging, you may want a pristine mirror. Check before replacing the old one; it may be handmade of thicker glass and have beveled edges, making it more economical to have the mirror resilvered by a professional rather than replacing it. Conversely, if you set a new mirror in an old frame, you may want to have it antiqued for an aged appearance; send it to a mirror company and have it done professionally with acid.

Antiques dealer Kathy Shorr rests a flea market mantel decoratively against the wall like a shelf. It's flanked on either side by mirrors set in some of the old frames she collects.

OVERLEAF:

The spaciousness of Donna Karan's modern house is accentuated by elaborately framed mirrors used as screens or placed about the room, where they add architectural detail. Salvaged bits from an old building serve as a base for the coffee table.

KITCHEN COLLECTIBLES

Some of Phyllis Lande Fairhurst's colorful Fiestaware is displayed in a corner of her kitchen along with a few pieces of Mexican pottery, some brightly hued aluminum glasses from the '50s, and a sleek vintage electric mixer that is still going strong.

T HERE'S SOMETHING comforting about kitchen collectibles. An old eggbeater or an Art Deco toaster is an instant reminder of the warm kitchens of childhood. Many old kitchen utensils are now more decorative than useful, but brightly colored bowls from the '30s still serve proudly in country kitchens; small electrical appliances continue to produce crisp toast and waffles; old-fashioned jelly glasses lend their charm to homemade preserves; even the old stoves, kitchen cabinets, and refrigerators that turn up at flea markets and yard sales can enjoy a new life in a collector's kitchen. And while a rare apple parer can command a price

of several thousand dollars, an old Mason jar, cookie cutters, or a handsome cocktail shaker or bowl are more than affordable. ◆ With such a wide range of kitchen-related items to choose from, wise collectors tend to specialize. Focus on gadgets like nutmeg graters, wire skimmers, or beaters and keep an eye out for the endless variations; hunt for toasters or other appliances that reflect the history of industrial design; or amass a handsome display of old spice tins with colorful graphics. Better still, search out old bowls, pitchers, and storage containers. They make mixing up a cake or a batch of iced tea more pleasurable while adding warmth to your kitchen. The enormous variety of objects luring collectors has led to a veritable library of specialized books. Since it would have been impossible for us to record all this information, we hope that you will use this book to discover some of the many options awaiting you at the flea market, then do further research on those that appeal to you most. ◆ From the turn of the century on through the 1940s and '50s, American companies produced a vast assortment of bowls, plates, pitchers, platters, and other kitchenware that was both colorful and practical. Some was destined strictly for the home, while other, sturdier pieces were designed with hotels and restaurants in mind. Pyrex and plastics brought an end to the proliferation of kitchen pottery, but a plethora of wares remain to be found at flea markets and yard sales. Here are some of the most sought after.

Bauer Ware
Bauer Pottery began producing flowerpots around the turn of the century. In 1932 they introduced Ring, a line of dinnerware distinguished by all-over concentric ribs on the bowls, cups, and rims of the plates, and glazed in cheery colors like jade green, royal blue, light blue, Chinese yellow, and orange-red as well as black and white. When World War II caused a shortage of materials for bright glazes, pastel colors were introduced.

Fiesta
Although prices have soared, collectors are still drawn to Fiesta's simple lines and sunny solid colors. Introduced in 1936 by the Homer Laughlin China Co., who also made the rather similar Harlequin and Riviera lines, it was originally offered in orange-red, cobalt blue, light green, and yellow, which were soon joined by turquoise and white. Dark

Country pieces of spatterware,

ironstone, and enameled tin are as collectible for their utilitarian appeal as they are for strictly decorative purposes.

The pie safe in antiques dealer
Alex Sigmon's kitchen houses part of his large collection of bowls. "It was designed to keep the bugs off food," he notes, "but it's great for everyday storage: You can see what's in it, but the contents are still contained."

green, rose, chartreuse, and gray were added in the '50s to satisfy contemporary taste. In 1959 a medium green, now the most expensive color, was introduced. Production ceased in 1973, but in 1986 Homer Laughlin reintroduced Fiesta in new colors: white, black, a darker cobalt, bright pink, and apricot. A greener turquoise, periwinkle blue, yellow, a misty green, and lilac came later still.

Lu-Ray Pastels

Introduced in the late '30s at about the same time as Fiesta, Lu-Ray Pastels were available as dinnerware as well as water tumblers, bowls, pitchers, and relish dishes or small vases. It reflected the era's streamlined design, interpreted in a more feminine combination of curves and soft colors called Sharon Pink, Persian Cream (a soft yellow), Windsor Blue, and Surf Green. Chatham Gray, a later addition to the line, was discontinued after just four years.

Watt Pottery

Originally a standard stoneware producer for clients like Woolworth, hardware stores, and gas stations, Watt's highly collectible kitchenware was put into production in 1935. This yellowware pottery was hand-decorated with appealing brush-stroke designs in bright colors: Some pieces done as premiums also had a stenciled advertising message. Since each piece was hand-painted, no two are alike. Reproductions are slightly smaller and sometimes in new shapes; the glazes are a different color; the tulip silhouette and the stems and leaves on the apples are also different.

Hull Pottery

From the 1930s to the '50s, Hull Pottery produced a great variety of commercial ware as well as art pottery finished in pale matte glazes and bedecked with flowers and ribbons. From that date on, the company favored shiny glazes like the one used in the dinnerware line known as Mirror Brown, which included bowls, casseroles with a duck or chicken as the lid, canisters, and trays shaped like gingerbread men along with standard dinnerware pieces.

Hall China Co.

Founded in 1903, Hall China is still going strong. They have produced an endless array of dinnerware, mixing bowls, tea- and coffeepots, pitchers, and casseroles for both home and commercial use. The most collectible pieces, all in a range of solid colors, are those made from the '20s to the '50s, especially teapots, bowls, and pitchers.

Thomas Rosamilia displays black memorabilia, one of today's hottest and priciest categories, on shelves in the kitchen. Some salt and peppers, syrup pourers, and spoon holders are in the guise of Aunt Jemima; other less traditional pieces have a Caribbean influence.

OVERLEAF:

An inveterate collector, Bobby Bant had the shelves in her kitchen and the living room side of the kitchen counter built specifically to house and display her vast assortment of Fiestaware.

DECO REVISITED

FOR PHYLLIS Lande Fairhurst, going to yard sales and the flea market is a Saturday-morning ritual. Her job as a producer takes her many places, but whether in California or Amsterdam, she hits the local flea market. One of the reasons Phyllis likes shopping this way both for her home and for herself is because the quality is often better than that of contemporary items. "I've always worn flea market clothes," she says. "You can wear them for ten to fifteen years, and they're recession proof. You always get your money back if you resell them."

Furniture, too, often holds up better. The small summer cottage she and her husband share on the edge of a bay is filled with her finds. "I can't buy any more, but I still go. It's a disease in a way," she admits. Even if she's not shopping for herself, Phyllis keeps in mind the preferences of her friends, buying items she knows they want if she stumbles on them at an exceptional price. She adds a small finder's fee to cover her effort as well as the risk involved in buying without a definite commitment.

Although she had envisioned a Laura Ashley cottage, when a friend presented her with a print of Marilyn Monroe by Bert Stern, the house evolved into an homage to the '40s and '50s. Flea market finds are mixed in with expensive pieces: For example, after investing in a pretzel couch, she was lucky enough to find two matching chairs at a flea market. In the dining room, vintage Heywood-Wakefield pieces are paired with an inexpensive cabinet with the same feeling.

One of Phyllis Lande Fairhurst's favorite

finds is the Art Deco kitchen cabinet she discovered at a yard sale. Holding part of her extensive collection of Fiestaware and other American pottery, it fits perfectly in the little dining nook off the kitchen, a perfect companion to the old enameled-top kitchen table from a used furniture shop. Vintage fabrics found at a variety of flea markets enliven the cushions on the banquette.

T HE IRON TRIVETS used to support cooking utensils on an uneven hearth in colonial times are both rare and expensive. However, after the industrial revolution, iron, brass, and bronze trivets in a wide variety of shapes and sizes were manufactured in generous numbers. The Victorians also fashioned fanciful examples out of wire, which may be more visually appealing albeit less sturdy. Other trivets were made from wood or ceramic tiles that do not conduct heat; silver trivets set on ivory legs were reserved for more formal occasions. All are still serviceable in today's kitchens and are often decorative enough to be displayed. ◆ At the turn of the century tinkers bent and twisted iron wire into everything from simple dish drainers and egg baskets to intricately crafted handheld toasters, trivets, spatulas, carpet beaters, and serving pieces. Wireware coated with tin better withstood the ravages of time, but uncoated pieces rusted beyond usefulness and were discarded. Mass production and more durable materials brought an end to the tinker's craft in the 1940s, but by then many pieces had been made, both here and in Europe, and good examples still abound, especially in France and England. Beware: Manufacturers are faithfully reproducing many old shapes like baskets, glass carriers, and postcard holders.

METALWORK

The wonderful collection of

wirework assembled by landscape designer Wallace Huntington illustrates the graphic quality of these practical but whimsical objects. Collections can be based on variations of one or two particular objects: Note the variety in the egg baskets and spatulas.

Trivets, cookie molds, rolling

pins, utensils, and other kitchen collectibles make an attractive display but are still easily accessible when hung on the wall.

Old graters are

recycled into handsome kitchen lanterns.

Seltzer bottles gleam like jewels in the window of Jill Gill's New York apartment. Once used extensively both in the United States and Europe, they are still in plentiful supply. As with other bottles, the deeper the color the more valuable the bottle.

BOTTLES

VAST NUMBERS OF BOTTLES in a great variety of sizes, shapes, colors, and designs show up at flea markets and yard sales, and the odder the shape, the more collectible the bottle. Early bottles were free-blown, but during the 1800s they began to be shaped inside molds. In 1903 machines took over much of the production. Embossed lettering appears on bottles from 1869 on. ◆ Collectors look for old milk bottles; canning jars; ink bottles; medicine, bitters, and poison bottles; soda and mineral water bottles (plentiful from the mid to late 1800s when mineral water enjoyed its first vogue); cologne and barber bottles; as well as whiskey, beer, figural, and historical flasks. An original label increases the value of any bottle. ◆ Most bottles are clear, light blue, green, or occasionally brown. Amber, dark purple, dark green, black, and milk glass are more valuable, while cobalt blue is best of all. Beware: While old bottles can turn purple from exposure to the sun, new bottles will take on the same tint when run through the machine used to iridize food. ◆ Flasks were made from the 18th century up through the end of the 1800s and came in a range of colors: the more intense the color, the more valuable. The Cadillacs of bottle collecting, flasks were decorated with a variety of embossed patterns or molded into figurals. Many reproduction flasks are available today, but even some new figural bottles like those from Jim Beam are now considered collectible and are certainly more affordable.

In Chris Mead's apartment, a vintage seltzer bottle has been transformed into a sleek lamp with a contemporary feeling.

A vast array of Depression glass at a dealer's booth at Brimfield.

ESPITE ITS NAME, Depression glass was made before the Depression and on into the 1960s, but it reached the peak of its popularity between 1920 and 1940. A twenty-piece dinner set sold for $2.50 and individual pieces were cheap enough to be given away at movies, in soap and cereal boxes, or as prizes for selling seeds. Occasionally a complete dinner set was offered as an incentive for buying furniture. The advent of the electric refrigerator and the huge popularity of ice cream created a demand for soda glasses and sundae dishes, as well as refrigerator dishes and items such as mixing bowls and measuring cups; juice reamers in different sizes for lemons, oranges, and grapefruits were also common. After the repeal of Prohibition in 1933, cocktail shakers and glasses, ice buckets, punch cups, and decanters appeared. ◆ The appeal stems from its wide range of feminine colors—pink, green, yellow—and the vast array of cut and etched patterns inspired by Art Deco, Art Nouveau, and flora and fauna. Lacy patterns date from the late '20s: Designs became heavier as the '30s progressed and were eventually inspired by Art Deco. And while the inexpensive production process left mold marks and bubbles in the glass, the intricate designs masked them well. ◆ Although originally Depression glass referred only to the pale colors made during the '20s and '30s, by the '70s collectors had expanded their collecting to include cobalt blue, emerald, amethyst, and ruby wares made in the late '30s and '40s. Some patterns also came in clear glass. Since vast quantities of these wares were produced, prices, except for odd pieces like cookie jars, butter dishes, and serving pieces, remain reasonable. ◆ Collectors often limit their search to one pattern or color or to a particular item like juicers. Remember that a lightly scratched piece is fine for home use but only a perfect piece will retain its value over time.

DEPRESSION GLASS

CARE OF GLASS

◆ Sudden temperature changes weaken glass; wash old glass by hand in lukewarm water with mild soap or detergent. Since minerals are the cause of cloudy glass, dishwashing detergents can also diminish the appeal of your glass finds.

◆ Don't display glass in a sunny window: The heat may cause it to develop stress cracks and sun can also discolor colored glass as well as any epoxy glue that has been used in repairs.

◆ If an old glass container has become cloudy, it may be impossible to make it clear again, but try filling the bottle or jar with a mixture of vinegar and salt and let it stand overnight. Rinse and repeat if necessary. You can also mix fine sand with water or denatured alcohol and swish it around until the fogginess disappears. Alternatively, fill the bottle two-thirds full of warm water; add two capfuls of household cleaner and the crushed shells of two eggs. Shake, empty, and rinse. If none of these methods work, you can do a temporary fix for display purposes by swabbing the inside of the container with mineral oil. The stopper will keep it from evaporating.

◆ To remove caked sediment from the bottom of a bottle, start by rinsing out with soap and warm water. If this doesn't work, fill the jar with vinegar and water and soak for a day or two, then rinse. If the sediment doesn't respond to this acid bath, an alkaline bath of baking soda and water will generally loosen it.

◆ If a stopper is stuck in a bottle, try loosening it by drizzling oil around the opening. If this doesn't work on an inexpensive bottle, ignore the warnings about change of temperature and put the bottle in the freezer for about ten minutes so the cold can "shrink" the stopper, then run warm water over the neck, which should cause it to expand enough to release the stopper. Take any valuable bottles to a professional.

◆ Don't store any liquid in glass containers: Even water leaves a line that may be impossible to remove. The acidity of wine is particularly harmful and one cause of "sick" glass. If an inexpensive glass has a minuscule chip on the rim, file it down carefully with a special file available in housewares stores. Expensive glasses, bigger chips, and scratches or broken stems and handles should go to a professional.

◆ To repair a broken glass plate or platter, spread a little epoxy on the break and put the pieces together. Allow the repair to dry at least six hours, then remove any excess glue with acetone and a single-edge razor.

COLLECTIBLE GLASS

THE SPARKLE OF household glasses at reasonable prices entices many shoppers. Most vintage glasses were strictly utilitarian, but manufacturers like Heisey and Fostoria also made well-designed, quality pieces. You're also likely to find glasses with various decal designs. Horseracing glasses commemorating the Kentucky Derby and the Triple Crown are especially popular and going up in value, as are prices of beer glasses and mugs. Other popular collectible categories include cartoon glasses, soda glasses, sports glasses, and those from railroads and restaurants. Watch, too, for Kraft "Swanky Swigs," which were introduced in 1933 to hold cheese spreads. On the upscale side, look for etched soda glasses from the early 1900s. ◆ When cocktails came into favor during Prohibition, as a way to blunt the strong taste of Prohibition booze, shakers were made of everything from glass and chrome to Bakelite and ceramic. Others were elegant works of art created by designers like Norman Bel Geddes, Russel Wright, and Rockwell Kent in Art Deco designs. ◆ Goblets, glasses, and serving pieces in brilliant cut glass, another Victorian favorite, passed out of vogue after the 1920s, but regained favor again in the '70s and are now well priced. ◆ Pressed glass, a machine-made substitute for cut glass, was developed in the 1820s, making patterned ware available to almost everyone. It was particularly popular during Victorian times, and again in the 1930s when five-and-dime glasses were designed for everyday use. Sets are more expensive than individual pieces, so collect different pressed patterns to mix and match. Many of these glasses are being reproduced; check the bottoms for signs of wear.

In Victorian times it was not

unusual to find six or seven different glasses at each place setting. Since matching glasses were not de rigueur in pre-Victorian days, any sets of twelve to fourteen will undoubtedly date since that time.

While glass cocktail shakers

from the 1920s and '30s are cheerful and inexpensive, those by the Chase Brass and Copper Co. in chrome and other metals are more collectible.

DESIGNED FOR LIVING

DIANA WHITE, who designs sets and interiors, began scouring flea markets and yard sales to find what she needed for her jobs. "Flea markets are a wonderful source of unique and inexpensive things," she says. "That's important when you have a low-budget job." Unless she's after a specific object, Diana starts each flea market foray by making a quick tour. "I look for something that's interesting to me because of its shape, form, and color. Once I get a major piece, I start to think about the period and continue looking for other items in that theme at markets and yard sales. But good design works regardless of the period," she adds.

In her kitchen/dining room, Diana White has accumulated vintage furniture as well as small appliances and dishes. The old refrigerator, while no longer used for its original purpose, does provide storage space as well as atmosphere. The sleek black '60s cabinets are elegant enough to work with the rather sophisticated dining chairs and table.

The Belgian gaming cabinet in another

area of the kitchen was originally used by hunters to dress the spoils of the hunt. Diana painted it bright green and added a small sink: Now it doubles as a handy bar with nostalgic but still workable examples of a blender, siphon, and ice crusher ready for the bartender.

FLATWARE

F ULL SETS OF flatware in sterling silver, silver plate, or plastic-handled stainless steel frequently show up at flea markets but can be costly. Don't rule out incomplete sets: Mixing and matching flatware has its own charm. If you prefer the more traditional approach, picking a popular pattern and collecting the pieces over a period of time is another, more affordable option. ◆ Searching for "your" pattern or working out a mix of patterns can provide hours of flea market pleasure. Coin silver, only slightly less valuable than sterling, was generally fashioned into very simple, traditional flatwear patterns that work wonderfully well with almost any style. ◆ More amusing is the colorful plastic-handled stainless-steel flatware so popular in the '20s and '30s. Bakelite was the best known of these plastics, but all were sturdy and were produced in a range of solid or patterned colors. Since this flatware was mass-produced both here and in Europe, it is still plentiful, especially knives, though serving pieces are harder to come by. Keep in mind that many reproductions are now on the market.

Silver
A more casual lifestyle and the lack of servants to maintain precious tableware have enticed many people to sell off much of their silver; there is a huge array of silver pieces at flea markets, especially in retirement areas like Florida, and both sterling and plate can be found at prices comparable to if not lower than those for new pieces. This silver is being incorporated into a more laid-back lifestyle ˙ by a younger generation who treat it with respect but not awe. Silver candlesticks might just as readily be found on the kitchen table as on a fine old sideboard. ◆ Among the best-selling pieces are the ornate silver plate pro-

Available in both brights and pastels, some plastic-handled flatware had a pearlized finish; others were translucent or inlaid with a design such as playing card suits; still others imitated tortoiseshell, wood, or ivory.

As an alternative to either sterling or plate flatware, consider airline, restaurant, and hotel silver. Frequently well designed, it is nice and solid in the hand and designed to stand up to the heaviest wear.

duced throughout the Victorian era and into the 1930s. Flatware is also a good buy. ◆ Tea sets, though not inexpensive, are always in demand as are unusual serving pieces. And like other areas of collectibles, silver made by a well-known name like Tiffany, Georg Jensen, or Cartier is more valuable than a comparable unmarked piece. ◆ In buying silver, remember to judge the value of sterling by weight as well as design. Worn silver plate can easily be replated, although some base metal showing through is not offensive.

Hammered aluminum,

mass-produced from the 1930s through the 1950s, was referred to as "the poor man's silver" and is now a hot collectible. It was fashioned, often by well-known designers, into candy dishes, bowls, trays, ice buckets, casseroles, pitchers, candlesticks, napkin holders, plates, cake plates, vases, and ashtrays.

Since most lunch boxes saw hard

use, condition is important: Minor dents, minimal wear, and slight scratching are okay, but avoid vinyl boxes that have lost their shape or badly dented or rusted metal boxes.

F OR OVER a hundred years, lunch boxes were a common sight in factories and schools, but the colorful models from the 1940s on have caught the eye of collectors. Originally made of steel decorated with decals, by 1953 the boxes featured lithographed designs. In 1958 vinyl took the stage from metal, but the metal boxes had the most colorful graphics and the greatest variety. ◆ Of the hundreds of designs produced over the years, collectors look for those featuring well-known cartoons like Bullwinkle, characters like the Lone Ranger, or entertainers like Roy Rogers.

LUNCH BOXES

Although both lunch boxes and

Thermos bottles are collectible on their own, a matching set is even more valuable.

ONCE BASKETS WENT begging at flea markets, but are now prized by collectors. The earliest settlers brought baskets with them from Europe, then shared basket-making knowledge with the Native Americans. At one time, basket-weaving techniques were also used to make such diverse items as fish traps, funnels, and cribs. ◆ Fragile materials and construction combined with hard use left many old baskets broken beyond repair, so collectors should ignore age in favor of a well-woven basket in a style that appeals to them. Numbers of baskets were turned out in Appalachia in the 1920s and '30s and are still being made there as well as in New England. Often the basket makers are of Indian descent and their baskets are identical to those made by their ancestors a hundred years ago. As a result, it is difficult to determine a basket's age. But you can look for wear on the bottom, holes where brittle sections have broken off, and a natural darkening of color. ◆ About half of all baskets are made of long, flat strips of wood known as splint. Originally splint was made by hand (indicated by thicker, uneven strips), but in the 1880s machines largely took over the painstaking process. Most splint baskets have a simple woven pattern; more complex weaves leave hexagonal holes to allow easy draining of liquids. ◆ In the late 1880s willow was cultivated especially for basket-making purposes, then turned into decorative items like jardinieres and planters, sconces, and bottle covers as well as field baskets and hampers. More than one weave was sometimes used in the same piece, or it was painted. Willow is also used for the well-known Nantucket baskets, which are still being made today and bring very high prices. ◆ Straw, especially rye, was the material of choice for German immigrants who sewed the grass into long strips that were then coiled into round or oval basket shapes. Coil construction is also used to make some regional baskets, such as southern pine needle baskets, Midwestern braided sweet grass baskets, and the abstract patterned baskets of the Southwestern Indians. ◆ Victorians were enamored of fanciful baskets that combined sweet grass with willow in complex dimensional designs; they are just as charming today.

Although antique baskets are rare and pricy, a variety of newer pieces are plentiful. They make decorative containers for flowers, books, magazines, and more, and help keep clutter organized.

BASKETS

GRANITEWARE

UNLIKE SOBER CAST iron, the graniteware that began appearing in American kitchens in the late 1800s was both light and colorful. It was also cheaper and easier to clean. Mass production and wide distribution sent millions of pieces into American kitchens between the 1870s and the 1930s. Europeans were also making highly decorative enameled articles during those years, including many with painted decorations, increasing the supply available today. ◆ Intended primarily for the kitchen and bath, there are graniteware colanders, pie plates, muffin cups, pots, dishpans, footbaths, coffee- and teapots, pitchers, canisters, pails, Bundt pans, basins, slop pots, and more. The least interesting and generally least expensive pieces had a solid gray finish; colorful blue, red, purple, green, or brown swirls on white are most collectors' favorites. In Europe manufacturers also imposed a chicken-wire pattern over mottled grounds, used bold checkerboard patterns, or shaded the background color behind a floral design. Although interesting shapes in pristine condition and the rarer colors of red, purple, and cobalt are expensive, many examples still exist for smaller budgets. Older pieces sometimes had a company name fired into the piece, but they can also be distinguished by their plain white interiors, heavier weight, and more random pattern. ◆ Any hard knock tends to chip the enamel finish, so many less costly pieces will be chipped or stained and should not be used.

Knowledgeable shoppers can often distinguish the age of enamelware by the weight and color. Chipped pieces, though less expensive and fine for display, are not safe for kitchen use.

Fanciful coffeepots like these at L'Isle-sur-la-Sorgue often turn up at European markets, while the more traditional blue-and-white pieces are more plentiful in the United States.

THE POTTED PLANT

GROWING UP IN the country, Rebecca Cole was influenced deeply by her grandfather, "a great gardener," and a mother who harbored a deep love of gardening. At eighteen, with ambitions of becoming an actress, she moved to Chicago, then New York. She longed for some greenery and began a garden on her windowsill and fire escape. Since she'd always been addicted to flea markets, she combined her interests and began collecting quirky containers for her plants: a sink picked up in the street, an old washtub or an old tin with a handsome graphic design from the market. Friends began asking her to create container gardens for them, and when their friends showed interest in her talents, too, a business was born.

The Potted Garden, based in a downtown New York store, does gardens, parties, and the simple flower arrangements that Rebecca loves to put together in some of her flea market finds. "It's more difficult to have to go out and find something specific for a job," she explains. She generally whizzes through the mar-

ket looking at what's available and making a note of the things she wants and can afford. "If it's not there when I go back, I wasn't meant to have it. And if something is too expensive I don't buy it: There's always another good one around the corner. Whenever possible I try to buy several pieces from the same dealer; generally he can give you a better price that way."

For Rebecca Cole, the color and texture of the containers become an important design element. "I like the incongruity and sense of humor of putting beautiful flowers in old printed tins that show definite signs of wear," she says. Whether at New York City's 26th Street Flea Market, in New England, or down south, Rebecca is always on the lookout for containers that have style and are reasonably priced.

In Rebecca's creative hands a somewhat rusty blue-and-white graniteware coffeepot becomes the perfect container for an elegant bouquet of tulips.

ELECTRICAL APPLIANCES

T HE FIRST ELECTRICAL appliances were introduced about one hundred years ago. Toasters moved off the stove and onto the kitchen table with the development of a wire that could conduct heat for the length of time it took to toast a piece of bread. Amazingly, many older models still work and have great style as well, making them an interesting and useful addition to your kitchen, though they have little resale value. Collecting a series of toasters, waffle irons, coffeemakers, or mixers is akin to assembling a history of industrial design: Well-known designers like Walter Gropius and Raymond Lowey created many of the prototypes. The numerous Art Deco pieces, in heavy polished chrome with Bakelite handles, are especially handsome. Don't ignore newer appliances such as steam irons, popcorn poppers, and toaster ovens. The original GE toaster oven featured a superb design in heavy chrome with high-quality detail. Although still a bit short on nostalgia, these more contemporary pieces are becoming collectible and are very affordable.

Early stoves turn up occasionally and, refurbished, can become handsome and useful additions to the kitchen.

A vintage stove and table seem right at home in Ellen O'Neill's wainscoted kitchen.

At Brimfield, a dealer offers an assortment of old toasters ranging from four-sided pyramid shapes to sleek Art Deco models.

Part of Jill Gill's
large collection of
brown-and-white transfer
ware fills the wall over the
kitchen stove and an array of
colorful old tins. Other
favorite bits and pieces, such
as colanders, copper molds,
and spoons, keep the display
from becoming too serious.
Part of her collection of
Victorian tiles has been
embedded in the original
white tilework.

USING AND CARING FOR
KITCHEN COLLECTIBLES

MANY FLEA MARKET finds for the kitchen can give long years of use, but may need to be handled with more care than modern nonstick cookware or dishwasher-safe glasses and pottery. Here are some hints for prolonging their lives and making them safer to use.

◆ Clean the outside of copper pots with a commercial polish or a paste made from lemon juice or vinegar and coarse salt. Clean the tin lining with soap and water; never use a harsh cleanser. When the copper starts showing through the tin lining of your pots, have them re-tinned professionally.

◆ Dry cast iron immediately after using or it will rust.

◆ Never use abrasive cleaners or steel wool on graniteware; it will scratch the enamel surface. Try oven-cleaning spray for heavy soil.

◆ To avoid chips, handle enamelware carefully. It's simple to wash it by hand, but it can be run through the dishwasher if protected from being bumped. Coat rust spots on unused pieces of graniteware with a thin film of oil to prevent further rusting.

◆ Stains on enamelware can sometimes be removed by boiling a mixture of baking soda and water in the pot; or soak stains on the inside or outside of containers in a mixture of vinegar or chlorine and water. Rinse thoroughly with soapy water and dry to prevent rusting where the enamel is chipped.

◆ Prevent rust on trivets and other cast-iron pieces not used for cooking by heating the object in the oven, then wiping it with linseed oil. The oil will be absorbed as it dries, leaving the piece with a nice finish. Another alternative: Wax the piece with auto or floor wax.

◆ Although strong enough for everyday use, don't put plastic-handled flatware in the dishwasher: The heat and detergent are liable to dull the shiny finish and loosen the joints.

◆ If a steel-bladed knife rusts, clean it with fine steel wool.

◆ Keep baskets away from dry heat, which can cause the splints or vines to become brittle and crack. Wash baskets occasionally with baking soda and warm water applied with a toothbrush, then dip the brush in clear water and go over the basket again.

FABULOUS FURNITURE

S COUTING FLEA markets and yard sales for large pieces of furniture is a great way to express your personal take on decorating and still be considerate of your budget. Once the province of eccentrics, aspiring artists, or college students, flea markets now attract shoppers of all ages and economic strata searching for an intriguing piece to use as a focal point for their decorating scheme. Mixing and matching furniture collected over a period of time gives a room more personality than one visit to a department store ever could, and slightly distressed finishes add to their appeal. The trick is to know what you like. Almost without

An old serving chest, found by Alex Sigmon in the basement of a grand old cottage, was painted an Ocean Country green, then topped by more flea market finds. The old coffee and tobacco tins are part of a collection that is sometimes used for Alex's doll topiaries (see page 28).

Hunt Slonem's collection of Gothic Revival chairs includes one truly fine antique mixed in with flea market finds, each purchased for less than $100.

exception, pieces that "speak to you" will be compatible. ◆ Traditionalists will delight in reproductions of classic styles made from the last quarter of the 19th century on; those from the early part of this century turn up frequently. Dismissed as mere used furniture, they are actually well made, frequently handsome, and usually well priced. Others might prefer overstuffed upholstery from the '30s or wonderful bamboo and rattan pieces from the '40s. ◆ As earlier furniture becomes scarcer, some collectors have switched their focus to the '50s, especially classic pieces by name designers or their look-alikes. Old office and hotel furniture as well as metal medical cabinets and tables with clean, simple lines are also showing up in some very trendy interiors. ◆ Within reason, furniture with stains or minor damage can be rehabilitated. Most wood furniture can be refinished, but consider just polishing over the imperfections that give the piece a sense of history and age. Painted finishes can be spruced up rather than redone. After all, distressed finishes are popular these days. Don't be discouraged by worn upholstery; re-covering or slipcovering is not difficult, and throwing a wonderful old quilt, Marseilles spread, or a paisley over a chair or sofa hides a multitude of sins. Vintage beds, even whole bedroom sets, are also excellent buys.

An endless array of country cabinets sit on the fields at Brimfield awaiting the onslaught of dealers and collectors. More informal pieces like these generally outnumber the classics at this market.

Jill Gill lightened

up a heavy Victorian cabinet

with a coat of white paint.

It's a handy repository for

her eclectic collection of

pitchers, plates, and platters.

During the Victorian Age, a variety of furniture styles reflective of the period's fondness for ornamentation appeared:

Gothic Revival
From the 1830s to the 1850s, a version of Gothic Revival furniture modeled after the arches and carvings in Gothic churches appeared. There was little upholstery.

Rococo Revival
Overlapping with Gothic Revival, Rococo Revival prevailed from 1845 to 1865. Ornately carved fruits and flowers gave the furniture a French feeling.

Renaissance Revival
was popular from 1850 to 1875 and is best known for the massive beds, some with headboards as tall as 8 feet, and large dressers with carved wooden pulls.

Eastlake Victorian
Toward the end of the Victorian period, from 1870 to 1900, the makers of the simple rectilinear furniture known as Eastlake Victorian eschewed ornate carvings for simpler decorations of contrasting wood colors and incised lines, sometimes rubbed with gold.

Two other styles that originated during Victorian times remain popular today.

Colonial Revival,
the best known, began in 1876 and continued into the 1930s. Less expensive and better made than today's reproductions, it was based on copies of 18th-century furniture, such as Sheraton, Hepplewhite, and Chippendale.

Golden Oak
was heavy oak furniture mass-produced from 1880 to 1920. Available in both dark and light finishes, the asymmetrical cabinets, chests, rolltop desks, and claw feet dining tables are familiar to those who frequent flea markets.

The distressed white paint finish on the Victorian dresser in Berns Fry's bedroom gives it a more casual air, but it retains enough presence to mix happily with the gilded Empire style side chair.

WHIMSICAL FURNITURE

A whimsical
clothespin folding

table that doubles as a bar is
among Ellen O'Neill's favorite
pieces. "I always wonder
who thought of such an
ingenious thing. I'm intrigued
by their mind and would like
to have this person as a
friend," she says.

F ROM THE CIVIL WAR on, ordinary people created whimsical bits of furniture out of an amazing variety of readily accessible materials. Wooden spools were especially popular: They were joined together to make table legs or edgings, and these whimsical pieces are still fairly common finds today. Old bottle caps were also recycled as furniture. At a big flea market a sharp eye is sure to turn up a bottle cap mirror or picture frame as well as small tables where the caps are a major or minor part of the design. And cigar boxes were carved into pieces and reassembled in intricate three-dimensional designs known as tramp art. Although primarily used for small boxes and frames, this decorative technique was occasionally worked into entire pieces of furniture.

In another corner
of the living room
Ellen has a spool table that
was probably made in the
1890s when making furniture
from discarded spools was a
favorite Victorian pastime.

AN IRREVERENT STYLE

WHEN SHE GOES to flea markets, auctions, and estate sales, this Long Island antiques dealer, a co-owner of Ruby Beets, is always looking for pieces that project a sense of wit and joie de vivre. She shows the same style in her 1839 center Cape, once home to a lima bean and watermelon farmer.

"In putting together a room," she explains, "I'm irreverent about periods and style. Period and provenance don't matter." Combining what she likes in a casual, informal way, she was one of the first to embrace distressed painted furniture, which she finds "humanizing and comforting," and she likes a piece that betrays the maker's hand, whether it's a simple spool table or an ornate shell mirror.

Ruby Beets, the shop she runs with a friend, also pioneered in "machine-age furniture," metal pieces painted with a woodgrain pattern, that were made

for hotels and institutions. "I bought my first piece at a field auction and had it stripped," she says. Now a handsome chest holds clothes in the master bedroom. "It's a great counterpoint to peeling country furniture—contemporary-looking but still old." This type of metal furniture, along with medical cabinets and other industrial pieces, is now one of the hottest flea market items. That she was able to spot this trend early on is testament to her sophisticated eye and eclectic taste.

An oversized cabinet that once may have resided in the kitchen of a grand old home now houses pottery and books.

The updated "machine-age" chest coexists easily with a Victorian metal bed.

OVERLEAF:
By using traditional pieces with a slightly worn air, the owner has given the living room an elegant but inviting feeling. The pillows are covered with some of the vintage fabrics she collects.

INSPIRED BY NATURE

ALEX SIGMON and Alexander Jakowec are inspired by the natural greens of Long Island's fields and trees and the soft blues of its sky and water. Both in the house and in the antiques store they share, walls and furniture are painted in this palette. On trips to flea markets and yard sales Alex turns up everything from painted furniture to pottery in these colors. "I like to think of what we do as 'Ocean Country,'" he says. "People here are surrounded by both fields and ocean. I like to bring those colors into the house; it's like bringing nature inside."

Alexander looks for furniture and accessories with a whimsical side, "but they're all things of use, not just decorative," he explains. "And I like mixing disparate pieces like a romantic gilded mirror and draped cloths with country. It breathes new life into once-fine things that may no longer be so fine." His attitude reflects the simple ethics of life in his grandmother's country cottage, where everything was used, reused, and recycled.

A pale Ocean Country wall serves as a backdrop for the almost sculptural shapes of a collection of chairs.

Old coverlets hang on the line behind an Adirondack chair painted in one of Alex Sigmon's signature colors. A folk art bird house rests on the side table.

In a corner of the dining room an old country table holds a napkin-filled wire basket and a drabware bowl with a collection of Alexander Jakowec's personal treasures.

OUNTRY PEOPLE HAVE always made unsophisti-
cated renditions of the most popular styles of the day,
and to modern eyes these pieces have as much allure
as the genuine article. Since most of this country furniture
was destined to be painted, it was frequently made from mis-
matched wood. A simple paint job generally sufficed, though an exotic wood-grain finish was sometimes used to add importance to a simple piece. Good country furniture, especially with original paint, is now scarce and expensive, but many pieces with a country look can still be found. Bleached pine or painted ladder-back chairs, trestle tables, corner cupboards, pie safes, benches, chests, end tables and more from the turn of the century have enormous appeal even when the finish is distressed. Many beds, dressers, and armoires have survived from the servants' quarters.

COUNTRY FURNITURE

These simple country dining

chairs at Brimfield are quite handsome, although probably reproductions.

A collection of colorful stools

is stacked decoratively in a corner of Berns Fry's home, ready to be put into use as extra seating when the need arises.

An assortment of country chairs

are gathered around the table in Berns Fry's dining room. An old weather vane on the table is one of his architectural collectibles. Pieces of American pottery rest on the country cabinet.

A PASSION FOR WHITE

MARY BALTZ'S TALENT for putting things together was honed as a visual display director for a major store, as a decorator, and now as an editor of *Victoria* magazine. But nowhere is it more evident than in the house she shares with her husband and daughter on Long Island. Charming, comfortable, and romantic, the entire house was furnished without one trip to a department store.

Whenever she sees something appealing, Mary buys it and stockpiles it in the basement to use at some future date for a decorating job or in her own house. "I like moving things around, changing things," she says. Decorating with a palette of whites allows her to combine disparate pieces harmoniously: chairs, most of which were bought for ten dollars or less, are dressed in white linen; chests, tables, and other furniture are painted white; and beautiful old white linens are pressed into service as pillow covers, curtains, and table coverings.

Over the years she's discovered that it pays to be flexible. A

handsome old cabinet was being ignored at a yard sale because it was large and needed a bit of repair. Mary and Lawrence realized it broke down into two pieces and that they could do the repairs themselves. The owners were so eager to get rid of it, the Baltzes ended up hauling it away for free. Now the cabinet, repaired and painted white, resides in the living room where it holds Mary's collection of rose-patterned china.

By using a palette

of whites, Mary Baltz has unified an eclectic mix of flea market furniture into a tranquil, welcoming environment. Plants and floral china and prints contribute touches of color; vintage linens add softness.

A Victorian table

and chairs retain their vintage charm even when updated with a coat of white paint. Mismatched chairs add an interesting edge.

The Victorian hat stand in the entryway

was broken down on the bottom when they found it, but painting it white made any repairs easy to hide. Now it holds hats and umbrellas conveniently near the door just as it did many years ago.

20TH CENTURY

Art and Crafts

The Arts and Crafts movement in late Victorian England attempted to revive handcrafts and improve design by turning craftsmen into artists and artists into craftsmen. In the 1880s, some of its adherents spurned Gothic Revival for the simpler elegance of Queen Anne Style, but by 1890 most fell under the influence of Art Nouveau. Eventually, they opted for the austere solidity that became their trademark. The movement ultimately foundered because each piece was so painstakingly crafted and expensive, the output and audience were limited. ◆ American craftsmen were simultaneously spearheading a similar movement. They started with art pottery, but by 1910 were also producing simple, unadorned furniture commonly called Mission furniture. Its straight lines and lack of ornamentation were a welcome relief from Victorian excess.

Art Deco and Modernism

ruled design during the years between the two world wars. Great attention was lavished on the detail, materials, and craftsmanship of each Art Deco piece, and the importance of surface texture led to the use of exotic wood veneers like ebony, palm wood, Brazil, jacaranda, zebrawood, and violet wood as well as lacquer, animal skin, mother-of-pearl, and ivory. Cost was no object, but this elitism eventually led to the demise of Art Deco and the birth of Modernism. ◆ While it is often difficult to distinguish between the two, one major difference is that Modernists considered true beauty to be a result of function rather than decoration. Modernism was born when prominent designers integrated industrial materials into simple, unornamented designs for the home.

Heywood-Wakefield

There is renewed interest today in many of the mass-produced furniture lines of the '40s, '50s, and '60s, especially in Heywood-Wakefield. As the popularity of wicker faded, Heywood-Wakefield Co. turned their efforts to a line of spare, streamlined furniture in a varied range of blond woods. Like wicker, it was designed to be accessible to everyone. Interest in this simple, clean-lined furniture was rekindled in the '90s when the South Beach Furniture Company of Miami bought the name, logo, and rights to make almost exact copies of the '50s pieces. Look for vintage pieces with solid construction, dovetailed drawers, no warping, and unmarred finishes.

The cushions

of the '40s rattan pretzel chair, one of a pair Phyllis Lande Fairhurst found at a flea market, are recovered periodically but always in vintage fabrics.

Alex Exarchos

found these simple '50s chairs at the Miami flea market, then discovered a compatible table. He converted the door of a deep closet into a stylish bookshelf.

In Phyllis and Ray Fairhurst's dining room, the pale blond Heywood-Wakefield table and matching hutch were expensive purchases, but she found the Thaden Jordan chairs at the local church auction for just $25 each. Part of Phyllis's collection of Fiestaware (see page 113) is housed in the hutch; more resides in a flea market cabinet with a compatible feeling. "Although it's not Heywood-Wakefield, it echoes its simplicity," she says.

OVERLEAF:

At one end of Donna Karan's

living room, doors from the Paris flea market are simply propped against the wall, suggesting a room beyond. They are framed by weathered columns found locally and a carved coat of arms from London.

The Classics

During the '50s and on into the '60s designers and architects created a series of unique chairs that have become highly collectible classics. Many of these styles remain in production, but originals are less expensive than new ones. Period copies inspired by the most popular, though priced even lower, have less intrinsic value. ◆ Among the most notable of these classic chairs are those by Alvar Aalto, Arne Jacobsen, Verner Panton, Harry Bertoia, Charles Eames, Ludwig Mies van der Rohe, and Hans Wegner. Although not in the same league, the popular metal-framed, canvas sling "butterfly" chairs from that period are also being reproduced today, as are beanbag chairs, so keep an eye out for originals in good condition. ◆ In the mid-'50s, Paul McCobb designed the Planner Group for the Winchendon Furniture Co. in Massachusetts. It represented one of the earliest efforts to market component furniture, some of which featured sliding doors. It is now stirring interest again.

BUYING TIPS

◆ A piece with the original finish or paint is far more valuable than one that has been redone.

◆ Repairs lessen value.

◆ Beware of fakes: New pieces are sometimes made from old wood or created by combining parts from several old pieces. Old lumber is generally wider, and you can often see subtle marks left by hand-planing. Machined wood is flat and even.

◆ Most pine furniture was originally painted. Unpainted reproductions are now being made from old pine floors and barns.

◆ Sets of eight or more chairs were not common and are harder to find and more expensive than smaller sets. Consider mixing and matching chairs with the same general feeling.

◆ Complete bedroom sets are more expensive than separate pieces.

◆ Watch out for deliberate wear or damage. If you suspect that wear has been faked, use a magnifying glass to check. Old worn spots will be smooth and weblike; those that have been created by sanding often show signs of parallel lines under a magnifying glass.

◆ When buying large pieces like chests, armoires, and cupboards consider both utility and appearance. Check the size: Old pieces are often larger than modern pieces.

◆ To house a TV, a cupboard must be 20 to 23 inches deep. If you fall in love with one that's too shallow, remove and store the original back, replace it with plywood, and cut a hole out of the plywood to accommodate the TV.

◆ Look at the insides, backs, and legs of a piece carefully. Question added stains and paints as well as odd holes, which may suggest something was removed.

◆ The following help determine the age of a piece of furniture:

Sun bleach marks on one side of a piece or on a tabletop are hard to fake.

Wood shrinks with the grain, so an old round table will be 1 inch less in one direction.

Newer pieces often have a plywood drawer bottom.

Phillips screws were not used until the 1930s.

Machine-cut dovetails indicate a piece was made after 1840.

Dovetails, dowels, and pegs indicate an early piece.

OFFICE FURNITURE FROM the turn of the century on is now furnishing some of the trendiest living and dining rooms. From 1900 to the '30s, many of the wooden pieces were inspired by the Mission style: simple, straightforward, and unembellished. With the current revival of interest in that period, these pieces are an inexpensive way to achieve the look. ◆ By the '40s and '50s, heavy wooden pieces had given way to modern aluminum and wood chairs.

OFFICE FURNITURE

Shaw-Walker, a company organized in 1899 to make filing card systems, eventually added a line of lightweight but sturdy classic office furniture. From 1946 to 1959 they manufactured ergonomically Correct Seating chairs. In 1989 the business was acquired by Westinghouse and made part of the Knoll group, where it continues to produce office systems furniture. Since many people aren't tuned in to this furniture yet, it's still possible to turn up a real bargain at a yard sale.

As soon as she saw the first one, Rawley Sorman knew that old wooden office chairs would look great in her dining room. It took an entire summer to collect the six that, refinished to match, now seat dinner guests comfortably.

CARE OF FURNITURE

◆ Age and the dry heat in modern houses causes wood furniture to dry out and attract insects, so examine pieces for new holes and little piles of sawdust. Twig furniture, walnut, and beech are especially susceptible to gnawing insects; mahogany and oak are less vulnerable. If you discover signs of woodworms or other insects in a piece of furniture, spray an insecticide into the holes, repeating as necessary.

◆ Sunlight, extreme heat, excess moisture, and even air-conditioning can adversely affect the condition of furniture: the finer and older the piece, the more damage can be wrought. Problems such as deep water stains; flaking, peeling, or discolored bare spots; or a crazed finish need an expert's attention.

◆ Furniture should be dusted regularly, polished several times a year, and cleaned once a year. Varnish and lacquer finishes call for wax; painted finishes and unfinished pine look handsome with a wax finish, too, but most dry, unsealed wood is best cleaned and lubricated with a mixture of equal parts vinegar, turpentine, and boiled linseed oil. For a more traditional finish, substitute shellac for the vinegar. Never use oil and wax on the same piece.

◆ To wax, dampen a soft cloth with mineral spirits and test a small unseen spot. If it doesn't harm the finish, clean the entire piece thoroughly to remove dirt and old wax, rubbing with the grain or in a circular motion. Refold the cloth often to expose a clean surface, and continue until no more dirt is picked up. Let the surface dry, then buff it with a clean cloth. Using a clean cloth, apply paste furniture wax and let it set for thirty minutes, then polish in the direction of the grain. The faster you polish, the more the wood will glow. Don't use liquid, cream or aerosol polishes every week; they can eventually cause damage.

◆ To diminish the appearance of fine scratches, clean with a solvent and rewax. If this doesn't work, rub the finish with ultrafine steel wool soaked in boiled linseed oil to spread the existing finish over the scratches.

◆ Major scratches can be minimized but not banished by filling them in with a matching touch-up stick or shoe polish, then polishing.

◆ Perk up a dull finish on an old piece by washing it with a mild soap like Murphy's Oil Soap. Rinse to remove the soap, but don't allow any water to remain on the surface. Air dry thoroughly. This cleans away dirt and grime but not the polish. Rewax if necessary.

◆ To clean a varnished finish, make a mixture of ⅓ oil and ⅔ benzene. Saturate a 00 steel wool pad with the mixture, squeeze it out, and rub the surface to remove dirt, water marks, and wax. Wipe the surface with cheesecloth until no more dirt comes up. Dip fresh cheesecloth in alcohol and remove from the surface any film left by the benzene.

◆ A sagging cane seat can often be restored to its original tautness by setting several heavy wet cloths on it overnight.

◆ Dents in wooden furniture can be raised by filling the hole with a few drops of water, then heating the end of a flathead screwdriver in a flame until it is very hot. Dip the end of the hot screwdriver in the water: It will boil and raise the grain of the wood.

◆ Small, shallow burns can be fixed by rubbing gently over the mark with a dry piece of 0000 steel wool wrapped around your finger.

◆ To remove the white rings caused by setting a hot or a wet dish on waxed furniture, rub a thin layer of mayonnaise over the spot and then rub it gently with ultrafine steel wool. Or rub lightly with denatured alcohol or turpentine, then wipe dry with a cloth.

◆ Many old flea market tables have a warped top or leaf. To straighten it out, try putting the warped surface, concave side down, on the grass early in the morning of a humid day. The heat of the morning sun along with the moisture should straighten it out in about thirty minutes.

INSTANT AGING

THE LOOK OF AGED, distressed paint, like the subtly colored paint finish on the cabinet in John Derian's living room, is easy to mimic on a country piece using this simple technique.

MATERIALS

2 colors of latex paint (enough to cover the piece)
Paraffin
Putty knife
Medium-grade sandpaper
Matte water-soluble clear polyurethane (optional)
Burnt umber pigment or acrylic artists' paint (optional)

1. Start with a piece of furniture prepared for painting. Apply 2 coats of the background paint (this will be seen only where the paint flakes off), allowing each to dry thoroughly.

2. Carefully apply softened paraffin on the spots where you want the top coat to "peel." Apply a coat of the second paint and allow it to dry. Using a putty knife, carefully scrape off the underlying paraffin, allowing the undercoat to show through. (For a more complex finish, use 3 colors of paint. Apply wax over both the first and the second, then continue as below.)

3. Add more wear by sandpapering with the grain of the wood. Concentrate on the edges where normal wear would have occurred, rubbing away the top coat or going through the base coat as well. You can also soften and extend the flaked areas.

4. The project can be left as is, or if you want to protect it, apply a coat of polyurethane. For an antique look, add a touch of burnt umber to the polyurethane.

the CHINA TRADE

O NCE MAN DISCOVERED that clay could be shaped into bowls, jars, and plates, he began making containers for food, water, and other necessities of life. The pieces varied from the most utilitarian pottery to the finest china, depending on the particular type of clay used, the process, and the maker's skill. All are worthy quarry for the collector. ◆ Although fine old porcelain is generally found in antiques shops, more affordable finds abound at flea

Shelves above
Ellen O'Neill's
sink hold an assortment of
flea market treasures—bowls,
pitchers, tin canisters, tin
carriers, and even one of
the signs she likes so much—
in her favored shades of
blue, white, and green. A
large painted metal container
doubles as a garbage can.

markets and yard sales. Elegant wedding band china, charming transfer ware, sturdy stoneware, art pottery, and dinnerware from the '30s are just a few of the choices, with prices reflecting demand and condition. Some collectors concentrate on teacups, pots, pitchers, platters, vases, or plates, while others collect by color, type, or pattern. Sometimes an entire dinnerware set finds its way to market, but more likely you'll spend happy hours searching for pieces to complete the place settings needed. Inveterate flea goers agree that setting a table with a mélange of patterns can be very appealing, too. ◆ Don't overlook the decorative possibilities of flea market china: Hang plates on a wall or over a bed; mass vases on a mantel; or display your collection on shelves or in a cabinet. Ignoring chips and cracks in a piece intended solely for display often enables you to buy a pitcher or bowl that would be prohibitively expensive in mint condition. Even a big hole in the side of a pitcher is invisible when it's against the wall. Keep an eye out, too, for inexpensive broken china: By gluing and grouting the shards to any ordinary object, you can create a trendy and attractive piece of pique assiette. ◆ Since most art pottery was marked, unmarked pieces are considerably less valuable. Consequently, your chances of finding a bargain are much better if you are simply collecting for the pleasure of owning a handsome object rather than looking for marked pieces as an investment.

A collection of blue-and-white

china is displayed in Emelie Tolley's dining room. Color unites such diverse pieces as Asian Pheasant, ironstone patterns by Enoch Wood, Delft, and wares from the Middle East and Asia.

Blue-and-White china of all kinds is very collectible. Most beloved are the many variations on the popular Blue Willow pattern with its Chinese landscape. The first hand-painted English adaptations of patterns from earlier Chinese imports were made in 1760. ◆ About twenty-five years later, transfer printing replaced hand-painting and versions of the design were sold to potteries such as Staffordshire, Spode, Wedgwood, and Copeland. Although the early pieces are pricey (and a better investment), American and Japanese versions are more affordable. Much Blue Willow was produced for American restaurants, too. Although almost all Blue Willow was in blue, Copeland made a red version with a butterfly border. ◆ Historical Blue Staffordshire also attracts collectors. Several English firms produced this ware, each using a distinct border pattern. Although the borders differed, all had a transfer of a city, landscape, or historical scene in the center. Originally produced only in blue and white or black and white, the wares were later done in brown, pink, lavender, or green as well.

Lusterware Charming and sometimes quirky, lusterware is a favorite of collectors. Its distinctive lustrous glaze can be silver, pink, copper, or gold. In some cases, a mot-

Pink lusterware is relatively

plentiful; the many patterns, including numerous variations of primitively painted scenes or delicate flowers, mix together harmoniously.

Leaf and shell motifs are among

the most popular majolica patterns. Reproductions can be distinguished by less detail, lighter weight, plain white bottoms, and hollow handles with a hole where they join the body.

tled look was achieved by sprinkling oil on the wet glaze. This splash luster is still being made. ◆ Considered quite flashy when it was developed in England early in the 19th century, lusterware was aimed at the masses and was always popular in the United States. Almost all luster was produced before the turn of the century, and the best of it before 1850. Sometimes the entire piece was covered in luster; more often sections were left clear for hand-painted or transfer-printed designs.

Majolica was out of favor for many years beore it regained its popularity in the '70s. Although this colorful pottery with raised designs has been made in Europe since the 15th century, most of the pieces found at flea markets

were produced in England or the United States after the middle of the 19th century. Victorians were enamored of the genre and American manufacturers soon began copying English designs and developing their own, but it's difficult to distinguish the origin of individual pieces. Because majolica has raised designs, most old pieces show some signs of wear, which don't necessarily affect price. Small plates and newer pieces of majolica are appealing and affordable, though old and rare cheese dishes and teapots are pricey.

Still affordable, Wedding Band

china was manufactured primarily in Limoges, then the gold bands applied in the United States. The pattern variations lend themselves to mixing.

OTHER CHINA COLLECTIBLES

◇ Royal Bayreuth figurals in pitchers, creamers, hatpin holders, humidors, candlesticks, teapots, and so on

◇ Lutz of Florida ceramics for '50s buffs

◇ Child-size dishes, especially complete sets

◇ Oyster plates, popular from 1860 to 1910, when Victorians clamored for special dishes for each course

◇ Ceramic liquor pitchers

◇ Hand-painted china

◇ Lady head vases from the '50s through '70s from Japan or the United States

MERICAN ART POTTERY from the last years of the 19th century and the first half of the 20th is high on the list of many who frequent flea markets. Originally art pottery referred solely to limited editions or signed pieces. Most were made on a potter's wheel and elaborately decorated. Glazes, an important part of the design process, ranged from multicolored finishes, through hand-painted patterns under or over the glaze, to a quieter matte finish. Other pieces depended on applied pieces of pottery, impressed designs, or decorative cutouts. Some potters followed the Victorian style by using Moorish ornamentation and lavishly applied flowers; others reflected the simplicity of Oriental pottery; still others followed the lead of William Morris to natural renditions of nature in an Art Nouveau style. One reason that this pottery has become so collectible today is its compatibility with Arts and Crafts furniture, which is enjoying a renaissance in popularity of its own. ◆ To the purist, the term "art pottery" refers only to the early pieces, because when American entrepreneurism eventually took over, it employed machines to turn the production of art pottery into a successful business. Although at first much of the pottery was still shaped and decorated by hand and even signed, standardized shapes, glazes, and patterns simplified production. ◆ Finally, even this minimal handwork was cast aside, enabling factories to produce thousands of pieces a year. Present-day collectors looking for more affordable wares have expanded the art pottery category to include mass-produced dinnerwares, vases, and planters. Because true art pottery is so diverse and commands such steep prices, a fledgling collector would be well advised to consult one of the many

AMERICAN ART POTTERY

A sleek modern

bathroom becomes a little warmer when Albert Morris adds his collection of white American pottery.

American pottery

in various shades of green is displayed on a green painted table in Berns Fry's living room.

Albert Morris gives a collection of McCoy pottery greater impact by limiting it to one color, a trick that also unifies the disparate shapes.

excellent books on the subject before embarking on major purchases. For the casual collector, brief descriptions of some of the best known follow. See also the chapter "Kitchen Collectibles."

Rookwood

Among the earliest art potteries, Rookwood is also among the most collectible and expensive. Founded by Maria Longworth Nichols in Cincinnati, Ohio, in 1880, the best work was done between 1890 and 1925, although production continued until 1960. Rookwood produced vases, tiles, trivets, bookends, candlesticks, flower frogs, and other decorative pieces. In collecting Rookwood, age isn't as important as the artist and the quality. In addition to any artist's signature, the pieces are marked with a joined reversed *R* and a *P* encircled with flames. After 1900 a Roman numeral was added to indicate the year.

OVERLEAF:

Antiques dealers

Alex Sigmon and Alexander Jakowec avoid clutter by grouping their white American pottery on the dining room mantel beneath a cluster of small flea market mirrors.

Weller Another major American art pottery, Weller began production in 1893 and turned out prodigious quantities of fine vases, lamps, jardinieres, umbrella stands, and other decorative items through the first two decades of the 1900s. The early lines, many of which were signed by respected artists like Fredrick Rhead, Virginia Adams, and Jacques Sicard, covered a broad spectrum of looks, from metallic luster finishes and silver overlay to painted or incised designs of Indians, fruits and flowers, dogs, scenes of Charles Dickens's stories, and more.

Roseville One of the few commercial art potteries that survived the Depression, Roseville began producing its wares in the late 1890s and continued its reputation for quality until it closed in 1954. Much of the late work was decorated with molded fruits and flowers. Earliest pieces were often marked with the name of the line and a circle containing the name Rozane Ware. From 1910 to 1928 an *R* with a *v* in the loop of the *R* was used, and from 1932 until 1952, pieces were marked Roseville in script or R USA.

McCoy Of all of the commercial potteries, the most recognizable is undoubtedly McCoy. Beginning as the Nelson McCoy Sanitary and Stoneware Co. in 1910, it made art pottery after 1926. In 1933 the name was changed to the Nelson McCoy Pottery. Best known for their cookie jars, they also made other kitchen- and dinnerware as well as figural planters and vases, many for commercial florists. ◆ Pieces produced from the '30s to 1990 used several different marks, but many were unmarked. Any marks were incised in the mold and most contained the McCoy name, although some early pieces are simply marked NM for Nelson McCoy. In 1990 the rights and designs were sold and some pieces are now being reproduced. They can be recognized by the date marked on the bottom and the paler colors. New cookie jars with a McCoy mark are distinguished by their smaller size and a poor finish.

Displaying pottery pieces of one color together, as Albert Morris does in a guest room, creates a greater visual impact.

The larger pieces of American pottery, like those in Albert Morris's collection, though harder to find at reasonable prices, make a stronger graphic statement when displayed: Witness the mix of blue jars on a table in the living room.

AN URGE TO COLLECT

LIKE MOST COLLECTORS, Albert Morris hates to leave a flea market empty-handed. That's one reason he began collecting American art pottery from the later years: The pieces were inexpensive and plentiful enough to assure a "find" at almost any flea market. Moreover, the shapes and colors seemed to suit his modern house perfectly. "The house is so big," he says, "and I wanted something that wasn't precious and wasn't furniture. These pots make an impressive display that's pleasing to the eye and seem right in a summer house."

Reflecting his interest in gardening and flowers, Albert began by amassing small planters and vases made by McCoy, but soon expanded to include larger pieces, some of which now house potted plants. Beginning with a group of pots and vases in various shades of greens, now displayed in one of the guest rooms, his interest shifted to collecting peach, blue, burgundy, and black and white punctuated with an occasional piece of yellow. His only rule: Accumulate

three pieces in any given color before putting them on display.

Black and white pieces are relegated to the black-and-white master bath.

An inexhaustible cook and host, Albert also buys bowls of every size. These are stacked within easy reach on a rack in the kitchen and include pieces from Bauer, McCoy, Fiesta, and others. Since his collection was begun, interest in this type of pottery has surged along with prices, but many inexpensive pieces can still be found, especially in parts of the country where interest hasn't peaked as yet. Contemplating his collection, Albert says, "Collecting is a bit like a drug until you get as many pieces as you want. You're always looking for the one that's cheaper."

Many pieces of McCoy

and other American pottery were originally made for the florist trade. Albert Morris's soft green flower pots contrast handsomely with stacks of National Geographics in a guest bedroom.

Morris's assorted bowls,

vases, and pots make cohesive collections when grouped on a lipped table, above, or graduated stand, below.

F LORAL-DECORATED china like Mary Baltz's from the 19th century to the 1930s and '40s is among the prettiest of collectibles. Watch for designs with floral borders and center designs made by Haviland or Staffordshire, especially those featuring roses, daisies, and violets. Chintz, named for its overall

floral patterns reminiscent of the fabric, is extremely collectible though expensive, and lends itself to mixing and matching. Several different English manufacturers produced its pleasingly distinctive shapes in the dainty, crowded floral designs of the late 1920s through the brighter, bolder designs of the '40s and '50s, all of which appeal to today's collectors.

FLORAL CHINA

At Brimfield,

a dealer offers a selection of sturdy dishes hand-painted with fruits and flowers. Cheerily nostalgic, they would be a lighthearted addition to any household.

When Mary Baltz was married,

her husband brought along his grandmother's rose-patterned Limoges china. It became the core of a burgeoning collection.

WHITEWARE AND IRONSTONE

S IMPLE SHAPES in pure white earthenware are easy to work into almost any lifestyle. In the early 1800s Mason began producing English ironstone. Decorated with colorful patterns for sale at home, it was left undecorated for export to Europe and the United States, where it became an immediate success and remained so until the turn of the century. In 1850 the French recognized the sales potential of this simple ware and started production of whiteware with a slight grayish tinge. American manufacturers followed suit in 1870 with a ware warmed by a touch of cream. ◆ Since customers preferred English and European imports, some American makers faked English marks on their ware. Collectors, too, neglected American ironstone until recently, making it the most reasonably priced. Like their English counterparts, American pieces can be plain or decorated with moldings, transfer printing, or handmade patterns. ◆ White restaurant china of a more recent vintage is also becoming collectible. The sturdy dishes in basic shapes are fitting companions to today's casual lifestyle.

In one corner of Ellen O'Neill's kitchen, wainscoting was used to create a corner cabinet to store the bowls, platters, and mismatched white and blue-and-white china she collects.

A STYLIST SHOPS

BEVERLY SILVER has trained her eye to see what's good and what's not in her years as a stylist, an ability that enables her to shop flea markets and yard sales with dispatch. "In my business I have to be quick," she says, "so I always do a fast overall tour of the market first and leave smalls like jewelry until last." She often arrives without any definite items on her search list, preferring to let her eye wander over the offerings looking for something that will capture her heart. If it does, another collection could be in the offing.

"I love the hunt," she says, "but everything I buy must have a function. And since I constantly change what's displayed on tabletops, I always have an excuse to buy more." Pottery is high on her list of collectibles, especially those pieces embellished with flowers.

One of Beverly's passions is barbotine, with its elaborate applied flowers. This process of adorning plates, vases, and other pieces with applied decorations originated before A.D. 300, and is still in use. Although many of nature's creatures, especially snakes and lizards, are typical barbotine decorations, Beverly restricts her collection to flowers.

Like many people, Beverly also collects pottery that looks like corn, the quintessential American food. The earliest pieces of this corn ware were probably produced by the many firms making majolica in the last half of the 19th century. These early pieces are rare and expensive, but potteries like McCoy and Shawnee made many pieces between 1910 and the '50s. Tankards, pitchers, mugs, and jars from the McCoy line can be identified by the designer's name, Albert Logan Cusick, on the handle. And if you find a piece with very curly husks, it probably came from Stanford, another Ohio firm.

The colorful hand-painted bean jars and teapots lined up in Beverly Silver's kitchen were found primarily in Connecticut, although they were produced in Ohio.

While the jars have a country appeal, Beverly's collection of French, Italian, and American barbotine is more elegant.

PROPELLED BY COLOR

In Ellen O'Neill's charming old house on Long Island's East End, one living room wall is covered with a collection of blue-and-white china plates and platters. Ellen bought the house because she was seduced by the space and the distressed chalky white walls. Soon after moving in, she decided on a blue-and-white decorating scheme for the downstairs rooms and gathered together the plates and platters she'd been accumulating over the years at flea markets and yard sales. They were not all in pristine condition. "I don't want museum-quality things," she says, "so the flea market is the perfect place to shop. I look for things with mends and patches, platters with cracks, imperfect things. They're not as pretentious."

White is the glue that holds everything together here. "It plays up other stuff," says Ellen. "Cracked ironstone, plaster chickens, anything painted white or in plaster is right for this house."

She finds that having a specific point of view while shop-

ping makes it easier to find things: on the field her eye goes right to such items as blue ticking, blue gloves, blue-and-white china, or white enamel pitchers with blue edging. As she works her way around the market Ellen takes a fast look for major pieces, then goes slowly on smalls, looking under tables and politely going through boxes while chatting up the vendor. "After all," she says, "you never know what they haven't hauled out of the truck."

One wall of Ellen O'Neill's living room provides display space for her collection of blue-and-white plates and platters.

Tucked into another corner is a collection of white ironstone bowls housed in a distressed cupboard.

TRANSFER WARE

Transfer ware was first produced in England in the mid-1700s, but the majority of pieces that turn up at flea markets date from the 19th century. Made by inking a copper plate with glaze, printing the design on paper, then transferring it to the surface of the ceramic piece, the patterns were far more complex than any painted by hand. Designs, generally in one color, depicted historic spots, sailing ships, faraway places, and more—all combined with intricate borders. ◆ Thousands of patterns were made by a number of potteries, first in creamware, then later on in sturdier ironstone. Generally printed in blue, green, purple, black, red, brown, or even yellow, a few pieces were done in two colors and sometimes a printed outline was colored in by hand. Blue is now the most expensive color to buy, but others, particularly brown, are still affordable.

Different patterns of brown transfer

ware mingle with an assortment of brightly colored salad plates, an eclectic mix of colored glasses, and deliberately mismatched flatware on Jill Gill's dining room table. The flea market also supplied the very collectible French café water bottle, the glass salt and pepper shakers, and the napkins, which were stenciled by daughter Tracy to make them more decorative.

CARING FOR CHINA

◆ Washing hand-painted or gold-decorated china in the dishwasher will take its toll on the design. Wash these pieces by hand.

◆ Wash prized porcelain and earthenware in warm water with mild soap. Extremely hot water can cause crazing and may dull the finish. Crazed china and pottery should also be washed by hand, as dishwashing will encourage further crazing.

◆ Wash art pottery with tile cleaner, attacking particularly dirty spots with a scouring pad designed for nonstick pans. Particularly dirty porous pieces can be soaked in a mixture of hot water with one cup of sudsing ammonia and a half cup of powder cleanser for one or two days. Rinse and soak in clear hot water overnight. If necessary, rub with a scouring pad and a mild cleanser.

◆ Avoid leaving foods that may stain in crazed dishes. If they become discolored, try removing the stain or mottling with a weak solution of hydrogen peroxide, distilled water, and a few drops of ammonia. (Do not use this solution on gold or hand-painted decorations.) Never use chlorine bleach: It will get under the glaze and cause further damage.

◆ Store plates and platters with soft cloth between them to prevent scratches. Felt can be cut to size and requires no stitching.

◆ Make cosmetic repairs on white pottery by filling small cracks or chips with opaque white nail polish. Make doing minor repairs on broken china easier by putting one piece in sand with the break exposed. This frees both hands to work on the repair.

◆ Repair a leak in a vase by sealing it both inside and out with clear silicone glue or by melting paraffin on the inside of the crack.

◆ Remove dust from figurines or relief pottery with a small artist's brush. Left untouched, it can eventually eat through and mar the finish of fine china.

◆ Keep decorated china, especially pink lusterware, out of direct sunlight to avoid fading.

◆ Hang cups in the cupboard or plates on the wall on plastic-coated metal hooks or brackets to avoid scratches.

◆ Mineral rings on vases can sometimes be removed by rubbing them with a damp cloth and some salt.

MAKING A PIQUE ASSIETTE TREASURE

INSPIRED BY THE WORK of Spanish architect Antonio Gaudi, pique assiette uses broken bits of pottery to create beautiful mosaics. Popular as a do-it-yourself, inexpensive way of transforming ordinary objects into decorative pieces earlier in this century, interest in the craft has suddenly soared. The wonderful thing about this technique is that it can be applied to just about anything and it's relatively simple. Here's how you can transform trash into treasure.

MATERIALS

Chipped, broken, or inexpensive china plates or saucers
Plastic or canvas bag
Tile cutter
Thin-Coat, a quick-drying adhesive for tiles
Palette knife
Grout
Powdered acrylic color for the grout (optional)
Flat-bladed putty knives in several sizes

1. Start by creating a good supply of shards. Place the china pieces in a heavy plastic or canvas bag and hit them with a hammer until they are broken into relatively uniform pieces of a good size for your project.

2. Work out a general design by laying out the shards on a piece of paper the size and shape of the object you plan to cover. Use the tile cutter to trim the shards to fit if necessary.

3. Apply a layer of Thin-Coat to a small section of the object with a palette knife, then press on the shards according to your design. Press them in so they adhere well. Continue in this manner until the entire piece is covered. Let dry thoroughly.

4. Mix the grout according to package directions and tint with the powdered acrylic to complement the shards if desired. Using a putty knife, spread the grout all over the object, working it between the pieces of shard. Wipe off excess with a damp sponge, then set aside to dry thoroughly. When dry, wipe off any grout residue remaining on the shards with a damp sponge.

At the Rose Bowl flea market in Pasadena,

California, pique assiette tabletops artfully combine tile shards with whole Victorian tiles or an attractive plate. A vintage lamp and ordinary metal candlesticks also benefit from a decorative dressing of shards.

RAG PICKERS

Ellen O'Neill has unceremoniously draped the old French bergère in her living room in blue-and-white ticking. Instead of a painting, an old blue-and-white-striped bathing suit top hangs on the wall, complementing the blue-and-white-striped decorating theme and enforcing the feeling of a seaside setting. An old shutter leans against the wall like a piece of art.

WHETHER THEY'RE SCOURING flea markets for the occasional still-affordable quilt, an old Hawaiian shirt, gently used damask napkins, or an old tie, aficionados of vintage textiles delight in the colors and patterns of these distinctive old fabrics. Attracted by a unique design or coloration, die-hard collectors even buy swatches too small for any practical purpose. However, most fabric items can be put to good use. The trick is to look beyond the original function: Recycle a colorful tablecloth into kitchen curtains, a lacy one into a bedcover; reuse draperies as slipcovers or camouflage

A simple blue-
and-white quilt

becomes a graphic headboard

in Ellen O'Neill's bedroom;

another rests on top of the

old chenille spread.

Displays of

relatively reasonably priced

quilts from the '20s and '30s

are among the attractions at

major flea markets.

Q UILTS, WHETHER THE elaborately pieced work of art of an expert needlewoman or an Amish-designed graphic, are eminently collectible. Though attractive to the eye, their original purpose was more utilitarian than decorative: Quilts were hung at windows or on walls for warmth or occasionally thrown on the floor to make a bed for guests. Even in the '30s and '40s, quilts were made to be used rather than displayed. These old quilts are now quite expensive, but if you consider them as the major decorative point in a room or as a piece of art to hang on the wall, the prices may not seem quite so outrageous. ◆ The most available and affordable quilts are those made from 1920 to 1935. Easily identifiable by their soft pastel colors and stylized floral or geometric designs, they were frequently based on kits or instructions printed in magazines and newspapers. Occasionally you'll find one with pencil lines marking the design, an indication that the quilt was never used or washed. By contrast, everyday quilts from the turn of the century were made from striped suiting and shirting fabrics in dark gray and black. ◆ Crazy quilts, or sections of crazy quilts, turn up rather frequently, too. Most were made from 1875 to 1900 using randomly shaped pieces of rich silks and wools that were sewn to a foundation rather than quilted, and embellished with elaborate embroidery. They were generally more decorative than functional, but Victorians sometimes fashioned them into table mats, pillow covers, ladies' robes, or large throws to drape over a sofa. If you buy a crazy quilt that is too fragile for everyday use, frame your find to highlight the embroidery and use of color. ◆ When buying a valuable quilt, check the condition, the workmanship, design, color, and the intricacy of the stitching: Fine stitchwork has eleven stitches to an inch (a magnifying glass can help you check the sewing). Although a worn binding is easily repaired, it's best to avoid quilts with stains, repairs, or uneven fading. Some less expensive quilts may combine old fabrics on the face with machine stitching, synthetic thread, and a backing of polyester batting. Less pricey quilt tops (pieced work that is not quilted) and individual quilt squares can be transformed into attractive shower curtains, tablecloths, pillow covers, or place mats, or framed and hung on the wall.

QUILTS

A SENSE OF STYLE

Upstairs in a bedroom, the green iron bed, a find at Brimfield, is bedecked with an old floral spread and pillows. "I like to keep the bedrooms as simple as possible," says Ellen.

The dining room is a splendid sample of how Ellen uses fabric to add style to the most mundane pieces.

A simple trestle table is draped with an old white cloth while blue-and-white ticking shades the windows and covers pillows. Dish towel fabric bought by the yard is stitched into simple slipcovers for old dining room chairs.

More striped fabric is draped over a canvas-covered armchair.

EVEN AS A LITTLE girl, Ellen O'Neill loved quilts. "I used to have calico quilt contests to pick out my favorite patch and my favorite design," she says. Now she regards them and other old textile pieces as artwork. "I'm not good with paintings or photos. They're too pretentious for me. I prefer to hang quilts and clothing—and I love thumbtacks," she admits.

Once the proprietress of a New York store where old fabrics and whimsical bits lured a devoted clientele, Ellen found all of her inventory at flea markets. "I started going to the markets, because I hate shopping in a department store and I love bargains," she says. "When I had the shop, the windows always had one piece of merchandise with a message. It might have been a cake box that sported 'I keep cake fresh' on it, but whatever it was, it hinted at a sense of humor, a sense of the time, and was a reminder that we're not the only clever ones that ever existed."

In the kitchen, Ellen kept as much of the old feeling as possible, a task made easier by her antipathy toward dishwashers and washing machines. The big old-fashioned sink, much like one you might find at a yard sale or flea market, was in good condition and provided lots of room for washing up and draining dishes. Ellen added a wainscoting enclosure for style as well as extra storage.

OLD CURTAINS in good shape can be put to myriad uses in your home. Alter them to hang at your windows, or revamp them into slipcovers, pillows, bedcovers, or even a skirt. Subtle printed linens and the brighter foliage, flower, and geometric prints from the '50s are among the most interesting. Don't worry about fading: The soft, sun-bleached colors are a large part of their charm. ◆ Napkins and tablecloths are other popular collectibles. Forget about having matching napkins, and assemble a mixed dozen or two of white damask or linen napkins from more elegant days or a colorful mélange of flowers, checks, or plaids to spice up a country table setting. Old dish towels, which were sometimes embroidered with initials, can double as big dinner or picnic napkins. Printed table and tea cloths from the '30s and '40s come in an assortment of lively patterns. Florals are the most plentiful and least expensive; fruits are more collectible. Maps, especially those of individual states, western motifs, geometrics, and ethnic patterns are rarer. While they make charming table coverings, they can also be turned into colorful curtains, skirts, jackets, tote bags, pillows, or even bedcovers. Patterns needn't match; just make sure the colors are compatible. Watch for reproductions, which can be hard to detect since a few washings age the colors. ◆ Old lace tablecloths are festive additions to holiday parties and special celebrations, but they can also double as a canopy for a four-poster or as a bed covering. On a smaller scale, embroidered, lacy, or printed squares add a decorative note atop a skirted round table or folded and stitched into a pillow cover.

CURTAINS AND TABLE LINENS

A splashy floral flea market print

separates the kitchen from the dining room in Alex Sigmon and Alexander Jakowec's Long Island house. The lamp atop the painted cabinet sports one of Alex's whimsical shades, a colorful mélange of fake fruits and leaves.

Vintage '30s and '40s tablecloths

like these offered at Brimfield are still charming, practical, and plentiful.

In Beverly Silver's bedroom, her

love of flowers is apparent in the vintage fabric pillows and tulip bedcover as well as the barbotine vase, hand-painted plate, and hollyhock painting.

PILLOW TALK

Thomas lets fabrics like those piled on his porch table inspire his novelty pillows. Some are decorated with buttons, others combine fabrics in an interesting way or are adorned with fringe.

Some fabrics that escape from the pillow-making studio add color and warmth throughout Thomas's house. Retro table linens curtain a cabinet in the bathroom, while vintage dish towels double as hand towels.

FEELING BURNED OUT from a high pressure career in the travel business, Thomas Rosamilia decided to move to the country and pursue a career as a housewares designer, making one-of-a-kind pillows from his collection of flea market fabrics. "I always had an affinity for old fabrics," he says, "and I used to buy them and stockpile them for no reason." Now, in addition to making pillows, Thomas sells some of his vintage fabrics to other designers for inspiration.

His flea market trips have now become part of the business. "When I go, it's like preparing for combat. I take premoistened towelettes, tissues for the Porta Potti, bottles of water, rain gear, an umbrella, tape measure, scissors, and business cards." Thomas goes directly to the back of the market and works forward because first-time dealers generally get the least choice spots in the back and their pickings are better. "I prefer to go alone," he says. "That way I can go fast and focus on one or two main themes. If I find anything else, it's luck." His advice to other shoppers: Buy it when you see it.

LD WHITE LINENS with their crocheted or lacy trims are always in evidence at flea markets. Most date from the days when Queen Victoria's love of lace inspired a fad for these fragile linens, and lace pieces were seen on tables, chairs, and other furniture throughout the house. If you find strong, undamaged pieces, these pristine white embroidered and lace-trimmed tablecloths, sheets, and shams are useful as well as beautiful. Pillow shams can be made into half curtains with a minimum of work or used to slipcover the back of a straight chair. Sheet shams, strips of embroidered or ruffled sheeting just a few feet deep that were tucked over the turned-back edge of plain sheets for instant glamour, are the perfect size to curtain a double window. Even the most ordinary table or dresser runners can lead a second life as bolster covers if you sew a seam up the long side and gather the ends around the bolster with a pretty ribbon. ◆ However you use them, these old whites will soften any interior, but they also require frequent washing and ironing to maintain their crisp beauty. Remember, though, that these old linens were never meant to be the brilliant white produced by the optical brighteners in today's detergents.

OLD WHITES

Chenille bed-spreads from the '30s and '40s are found in a variety of multicolor patterns or solid white-on-white and pastels. Designs range from Art Deco patterns to flowers, peacocks, and even cowboys.

In Emelie Tolley's pantry closet, a variety of old trims edge the shelves; vintage tablecloths are displayed and easily accessible on racks.

Mary Baltz delights in using vintage whites, often in unexpected ways. A length of old trimming softens the mantel and a too-pretty-to-store cloth is simply draped over the back of the sofa.

A WORLD OF WHITES

"I SHOP EVERYWHERE—thrift shops, yard sales, antiques shows, flea markets—and I look for everything. My basement is full of stock, so I'm constantly moving and changing things," says Mary Baltz. Among her favorite buys are old whites, which find their way into every room in her house. In the living room, pillows covered with a handsome collection of shams make the sofa an inviting spot to relax; a strip of lace softens the mantel shelf. Mary collects mantels (at the moment she has seven), which she treats almost like a piece of furniture. Their positions are changed from time to time, but they always add interest—and a shelf—to the room.

Her collection of old linens is prodigious, because she doesn't hesitate to buy pieces that may have repairs and stains if the price is right. "After all," she says, "I can probably get the stain out or hide the repair or I can cut them up to make pillowcases or shelf linings. And if I can't use it for anything, I haven't lost that much." She admits that the restoration and care take time and effort, but

over the years she's developed a few tricks that make it easier. "Since bleach turns linen yellow, I soak stained or yellowed linens and cottons in Rit Bright White for a couple of hours. Or I soak them up to several hours in water to which I've added a quarter cup of hydrogen peroxide. For a really difficult stain, I might use straight hydrogen peroxide." Delicate pieces are washed with mild soap in a lingerie bag; sturdy ones might be boiled for up to twenty minutes. When Mary prefers a pale ecru, she soaks the cleaned piece in tea until it's the desired shade and rinses it in cool water before drying.

Mary turned a vintage tablecloth into a bed throw in the guest room, adding a colorful decorative note while hiding an irremovable stain on the bedcover.

Old linens are on display even in the bathrooms, where an old piece of crochet work softens a shelf; pretty old hand towels beckon to guests; a nice old pitcher sits on a vintage doily; and a piece of old lace curtains the window.

RESSES AND COATS, Hawaiian shirts from the '40s, white cotton dresses and underwear, hand-painted ties from the '40s and '50s, old cashmere sweaters, western garb—all these vintage items are highly collectible. So are accessories like fine leather purses, belts, scarves, shoes, and even hats to be worn with vintage or contemporary clothing. These old clothes express the wearer's individuality and like flea market furniture often represent better fabrics and workmanship at more reasonable prices than you might find at retail. But you needn't wear them to enjoy vintage clothes. Try pinning a favorite piece to the wall, display them on hangers, or frame a particularly handsome piece. ◆ Hawaiian shirts, popular from the '30s to the '50s, have new admirers and bring big prices these days. Printed on a rayon that accepted colors brilliantly, they were so well made even the pockets were cut and placed to match the design. Hand-printed designs are the most valuable; but double-stitched seams, matched pockets, coconut or copra seed buttons, and "made in Hawaii" labels are also desirable features. ◆ Somewhat akin to these colorfully printed shirts are the bold printed ties from the postwar '40s that allow the collector a bit of self-expression. A reaction to the many years of drab wartime khaki, these exuberant ties expressed postwar

VINTAGE CLOTHES

At a Long Island flea market, vintage glamour is displayed most unglamourously on the dealer's van.

Vintage ties are plentiful, with designs ranging from strictly engineered patterns to hand-painted fantasies. They can be worn, used as belts, sewn into skirts, or even woven into a chair seat.

Button collectors look for picture buttons from the late 1800s, uniform buttons, painted porcelain buttons, decorated enamel or glass buttons, and Bakelite buttons from the '20s through '40s. They can be used to embellish pillows and clothes, framed in colorful arrangements, or transformed into mosaic lamps and vases.

Hat collectors are offered a diversity of treasures at most flea markets.

America's optimism. Many prints were engineered so they fell the same way for every tie, with the design tapering toward the top and focusing attention on the knot. ◆ Accessories can be among the most useful and interesting items to hunt for and are often more wearable than clothes. Beaded bags, from the simplest little unframed pouch to more elaborate fringed examples on a heavily carved and jeweled sterling silver frame, are especially collectible. The value and price depend on the general condition, the skill of the beadworker, the intricacy of the pattern, the color scheme, fringing, the size of the beads (smaller is better), whether or not it is lined, and the uniqueness of the frame. Buy only those in good shape, because restoration will most likely have to be done by an expert unless you are extremely skilled with a needle. ◆ Mesh bags, sometimes enameled in interesting designs, were the machine-made latter-day versions of bead bags and can be quite charming, too. Old alligator bags and designer bags from Hermès and other well-known names can be a handsome addition to any wardrobe if they're in good shape. Look, too, for tooled leather bags or the Lucite models from the '50s as well as opera or evening gloves, old hats with ostrich plumes or birds, wonderful old straw hats, and parasols or umbrellas with interesting handles or fabric coverings. Open umbrellas up before buying to make sure the fabric is in good condition and the mechanism works.

CLEANING TEXTILES

◆ Clean the surface of hangings and upholstery and slipcovers regularly. Tape a small piece of fiberglass screening to the vacuum to keep threads and fabrics from being drawn into the nozzle.

◆ Always check the strength of a fabric before washing and ironing so you know how much stress it can tolerate.

◆ When you buy an old piece of linen or cotton, especially white, soak it overnight in cool water to remove any old detergent and rehydrate fibers that may have dried out over time. Colored fabrics should be tested for colorfastness in an inconspicuous place by putting a few drops of water on them, then blotting with white blotter paper. Dissolve a small amount of soap in the water and repeat, then wash the soaked fabric to remove any invisible dust, dirt, or substances like perspiration that may discolor the fabric over time. Never rub; just gently squeeze the water through the fabric with your fingers.

◆ Never wash and dry quilts or other old linens in the washer-dryer. It's safest to send multicolored and dark quilts to the dry cleaner; other large pieces should be washed gently by hand if they have no major stains. This can be done most easily in the bathtub. Fill the tub with cool to warm water and add a bit of mild liquid laundry soap such as Dreft, not detergent. Do not use bleach unless it is absolutely necessary (see below). Lay the piece to be washed on a fiberglass screen and lower it into the tub. If it is very dirty, let soak for about thirty minutes, then gently squish the water through the fabric with a plastic sponge. When the water becomes cloudy, change it. Repeat until the water runs clear. A handheld shower nozzle is helpful for the final rinse to make sure all traces of soap are removed; otherwise it may eventually cause streaks. Press out any excess water, then use the screen to remove the fabric from the tub: Wet fabrics are heavy and lifting them without support can put a great strain on weak fibers. Roll the fabric in white towels to absorb any excess moisture, then dry flat on a clean sheet or mattress pad outside on the grass out of direct sunlight. To keep lace and embroidered pieces in shape, tack them to a corkboard covered with a polyethylene sheet with rust-free brass pins.

◆ To wash fringed items, roll them with the fringe inside and secure them with a string or elastic during washing to keep the fringe from tangling.

◆ Old whites can sometimes take a little more rugged treatment if they're in good shape. Soak yellowed pieces for thirty minutes before washing with a nonchlorine bleach like Snowy or Clorox II diluted with water. Treat any remaining stains with a detergent or mild soap on a cosmetic sponge, moving it gently up and down rather than rubbing. Wash strong pieces in boiling water if necessary. Rinsing whites with strained lemon juice or vinegar diluted in water, then drying them in the sun will also help to whiten them. Rinse again to remove the lemon juice.

◆ Silks, especially those with lace trimming, should be washed in warm water with mild soap. For very delicate pieces, try washing the fabric with dried soapwort root as museum curators do. It gives the silk a wonderful bloom. Simmer the dried root, available at herb stores, in water for twenty minutes, then cool and strain. Immerse the fabric in the liquid and swish it through the fabric. Rinse well, then roll the silk in a towel and refrigerate for several hours to strengthen the fibers.

◆ Iron old linens on a well-padded board. Press on the wrong side through a pressing cloth using an up-and-down motion rather than sliding the iron. To maintain the raised surfaces of laces and embroidery, iron them on a towel, right side first, then wrong side up. Press everything but silk while still slightly damp with a dry iron. Silk should be dry, and if you need moisture, place a damp cloth on top of the pressing cloth. If you can't press them right away, roll the linens in a plastic bag and refrigerate. Use starch only when necessary (never before storing), as it attracts insects and contributes to the breakdown of the fibers. However, most old whites look a bit limp without a touch of starch—just don't overdo it.

◆ Here are four ways to treat mildew, which can eventually damage a fabric. Test for any effect on color before laundering. (1) Dampen the spot, then apply a paste of mild soap and powdered chalk. Set the fabric in the full sun and keep it damp until the spot disappears. (2) If the fabric is strong, soak it for thirty minutes in a weak solution of all-fabric bleach. (3) Mix lemon juice with salt and apply to the spot and dry in the sun. (4) Sponge the spot with hydrogen peroxide, then launder.

DIRECTORY

ISTED BELOW are a selection of flea markets around the country that won't disappoint. Some operate every week year round, others seasonally, and some take place just two or three times a year. Since changes can occur, always call first to verify dates and hours.

NORTHEAST

BRIMFIELD
Rte. 20, Brimfield, MA
(413) 283-6149
◆ *Tuesday–Sunday three times a year in early May, July, September*

STORMVILLE AIRPORT ANTIQUE SHOW AND FLEA MARKET
Stormville Airport, Rte. 216, Stormville, NY
(914) 221-6561
◆ *One weekend a month from April to October*

FARMINGTON ANTIQUES WEEKEND
Town Farm Rd., Farmington, CT
(508) 839-9735
◆ *Second weekend in June, Labor Day weekend*

MULFORD FARM ANTIQUE SHOW AND SALE
Main St. and James Lane, East Hampton, NY
(516) 537-0333
◆ *One Saturday in June, August, September*

BOUCKVILLE ANTIQUES PAVILLION
Rte. 20, Bouckville, NY
(315) 893-7972
◆ *Sundays, May–October; extravaganza in June, August*

SCHUPP'S GROVE
Adamstown, PA
(717) 484-4115
◆ *Weekends April–October; extravaganzas*

RENNINGER'S EXTRAVAGANZAS
Noble Street, Kutztown, PA
(717) 336-2177
◆ *Extravaganzas: Thursday, Friday, Saturday of the last full weekend of April, June, September*

THE ANNEX ANTIQUES FAIR & FLEA MARKET
(26th Street Market)
Sixth Avenue, bet. 25th & 26th Sts., New York, NY
212-243-5342
◆ *Every weekend*

WEST/NORTHWEST

SANTA MONICA OUTDOOR ANTIQUE AND COLLECTIBLE MARKET
Santa Monica Airport, Santa Monica, CA
(213) 933-2511
◆ *Fourth Sunday of the month*

THE ROSE BOWL
1001 Rose Bowl Dr., Pasadena, CA
(310) 587-4411
◆ *Second Sunday of every month*

PORTLAND ANTIQUE SHOW
Exposition Center, 2060 No. Main St., Portland, OR
(503) 282-0877
◆ *Three weekends a year: March, July, October*

LONG BEACH ANTIQUE & COLLECTIBLE MARKET
Veteran's Memorial Stadium, Long Beach, CA
(213) 655-5703
◆ *Third Sunday of every month*

MIDWEST

SCOTT ANTIQUE MARKET
Expo Center, 717 E 17th Ave., Columbus, OH
(614) 569-4112
◆ *One weekend a month, usually the third*

SANDWICH ANTIQUES MARKET
The Fairgrounds, Rte. 34, Sandwich, IL
(773) 227-4464
◆ *Monthly*

CENTREVILLE ANTIQUES MARKET
St. Joseph's County Fairgrounds, Rte. M86, Centreville, MI
(312) 227-4464
◆ *One Sunday in May, June, July, August, October*

KANE COUNTY ANTIQUE AND FLEA MARKET
Kane County Fair Grounds, Randall Rd., bet. Rtes. 38 & 64, St. Charles, IL
(708) 377-2252
◆ *One weekend a month, weekend varies*

SPRINGFIELD ANTIQUE SHOW & FLEA MARKET
Clark County Fairgounds
Exit 59 off I70, Springfield, OH
(937) 325-0053
◆ *Extravaganzas one weekend in March and October*

SOUTH/SOUTHWEST

METROLINA EXPOSITION FLEA MARKET
7100 Statesville Rd., Charlotte, NC
(704) 596-4643
◆ *First and third weekend of every month; a spectacular the first weekend of April, June, November*

SOUTHEASTERN ANTIQUE AND COLLECTIBLES MARKET
Georgia National Fair Grounds, Perry, GA
(912) 471-8112
◆ *Four weekends a year; major show in the fall*

HEART OF COUNTRY
Opry Land Hotel, 2800 Opry Land Drive, Nashville, TN
(800) 862-1090
◆ *One weekend in February and October*

FIRST MONDAY TRADE DAYS
290 East Tyler, Canton, TX
(903) 567-6556
◆ *The weekend preceding the first Monday of the month*

ROUND TOP
3 locations, Round Top, TX
(281) 493-5501
◆ *Semiannual show first weekend of April and October*

THE KENTUCKY FLEA MARKET
Fair and Expo Center, Louisville, KY
(502) 456-2244
◆ *Almost monthly market with several extravaganzas*

RENNINGER'S FLORIDA TWIN MARKET
20051 Hwy. 441, Mt. Dora, FL
(904) 383-3141
◆ *Third weekend of the month in season; extravaganza in January and February*

LEXINGTON ANTIQUE AND FLEA MARKET
Lexington Center
Main & Patterson, Lexington, KY
(502) 456-2244
◆ *Eight weekends a year*

SCOTT ANTIQUE MARKET
Atlanta Exposition Center
I-285 at Jonesboro Rd., Atlanta, GA
(614) 569-4112
◆ *Second weekend of the month*

THE INTERNET

EVEN IF YOU CAN'T get away, you can still go shopping on the internet. Just typing in the words "flea market" turns up close to a million entries. Here are a few of the better sites to get you started.

http://www.the-forum.com
Easy to navigate, this website includes show listings.

http://tias.com
This major site for shoppers has a comprehensive book section in conjunction with Amazon.com.

www.curioscape.com

www.netcollectibles.com
Two on-line malls where you will find a wide variety of merchandise for sale.

www.maineantiquedigest.com
This paper's on-line site has a good list of shows as well as ads and other helpful information.

GUIDES AND TRADE PAPERS

SERIOUS SHOPPERS keep a flea market guide in the car and subscribe to the regional papers that list shows and auctions and prices.

Americana Flea Market Guide
American Vendors Association, Publisher

The Official Directory to U.S. Flea Markets, Ballantine

US Flea Market Directory
Avon Books

Goodridge's Guides to Flea Markets (regional editions)
Adams Media Corporation

Maine Antique Digest
Subscriptions: (207) 832-7534

Antique Review (Midwest)
Subscriptions: (800) 992-9757

Antique Trader Weekly
Subscriptions: (319) 588-2073

Antiques and Arts Weekly (The Newtown Bee)
Subscriptions: (203) 426-3141

West Coast Peddler
Subscriptions: (310) 698-1718

New England Antiques Journal
Subscriptions: (413) 967-3505

Today's Collector
Subscriptions: (715) 445-2214

INDEX